Transatlantic Liners

David L. Williams

PLYMOUTH PRESS

Ian Allan
PUBLISHING

CONTENTS

387.2432
W722t

First published 2000

ISBN 0 7110 2719 6 (Ian Allan Publishing)
ISBN 1-882663-50-0 (Plymouth Press)

Published by Ian Allan Publishing

an imprint of Ian Allan Publishing Ltd, Terminal House,
Shepperton, Surrey TW17 8AS.
Printed by Ian Allan Printing Ltd, Riverdene Business Park,
Hersham, Surrey KT12 4RG.

Code: 0007/B2

Acknowledgements

The successful completion of this book owes much to the
kind support and assistance I have received from the
following persons and organisations:

Christopher Balfour, Frank Braynard, Stephen J. Card,
Michael Cassar, the Cunard Steamship Co, the Deutsches
Schiffahrtsmuseum, Alex Duncan, Hapag-Lloyd AG, the
Imperial War Museum, Compagnie Générale Maritime,
William Millar, Moran Towing & Transportation, Newport
News Shipping Corp, Norfolk Shipbuilding Corp, Paul
Pälsson, Bjørn Pederson, the late Tom Rayner,
Rotterdamsche Droogdok Mij, Roger Sherlock, Smit
International, Southampton City Cultural Services, Table
Bay Underway Shipping, Stephen Tacey, Fabien Trehet,
United States Coast Guard, United States National Archives,
Warnowerft GmbH, World Ship Photo Library.

In particular, I am indebted to Philip Rentell and Ian
Shiffman who, as previously, helped me immensely with
high-quality, rare and unusual postcard views and colour
photographs of ships. Thank you to all those mentioned
here, and, anyone else whom I may unwittingly have
overlooked.

Bibliography

Bonsor, Norman R. P., *North Atlantic Seaway*, T. Stephenson

Braynard, Frank O., *Lives of the Liners*, Cornell Maritime Press

Hughes, Tom, *Blue Riband of the Atlantic*, Patrick Stephens

Kludas, Arnold, *Great Passenger Ships of the World*, Vols 1-5, Patrick Stephens

Miller, Bill, *The Last Atlantic Liners*, Conway Maritime Press

Roper, *The Atlantic Conference, 1921-1939*

Vernon Gibbs, Cdr C. R., *Western Ocean Passenger Lines and Liners*, Brown Son & Ferguson

Williams, David L. & de Kerbrech, Richard P., *Damned by Destiny*, Teredo Books

Williams, David L. & de Kerbrech, Richard P., *Cunard White Star Liners of the 1930s*, Conway Maritime Press

Williams, David L., *Liners in Battle Dress*, Conway Maritime Press

Williams, David L., *Wartime Disasters at Sea*, Patrick Stephens

Williams, David L., *Glory Days: Cunard*, Ian Allan Publishing

Wilson, R. M., *The Big Ships*, Cassell

INTRODUCTION

To attempt to write a descriptive account of something as richly diverse as the transatlantic passenger shipping trade in just 112 pages, even just the 50-year segment of its history from 1920, is a challenge of immense proportions. There is so much to relate: the ships, of course, the lines, the social aspects of Atlantic travel, the many events and incidents and so on. Fortunately, in this book, it is not the intention to deal with the subject in some novel way, to provide the reader with some hitherto unknown information. The story of the transatlantic liners, like a popular walk, has been well trodden over the years and the reader will find few surprises in the pages that follow. Instead, this is intended as a celebration in text and pictures, many in colour, of an elegant and evocative mode of travel now, regrettably, condemned to history. Between 1920 and 1970, it blossomed in its all too brief but glorious peak only rapidly to wither and die.

The shipping route across the Atlantic, connecting the old nations of Europe with the newly independent countries of North America, has been the most important of the world's ocean highways since virtually the day when the first settlements were colonised. From the mid-19th century, as regular steamship schedules were increasingly established, it was destined to become the scene of the most intense shipping rivalry as the passenger trade rapidly grew. Across its vast, inhospitable expanse, the greatest values of cargoes, the wealthiest of businessmen and the greatest numbers of immigrants and tourists were transported. As the showcase arena for the ascendant passenger shipping trade, the Atlantic route was at the vanguard of technology and development. It was the route on which the biggest, finest, fastest, most commodious and most innovative passenger vessels were progressively introduced as the competing operators vied to secure the lion's share of the traffic.

Like microcosms of society, the passenger complements of the liners plying the Atlantic represented all walks of life. Occupying First-class staterooms were the wealthy and fortunate and the well-heeled magnates of industry, all from

the upper echelons of society. Among them were those of 'Old World' prosperity as well as those who had secured their fortunes in the powerhouse economy of the United States and who were now able to enjoy the pleasures of travel abroad in Europe from where the majority had originated.

Down below, in Steerage and other lower grades of accommodation, were the less affluent passengers as well as the countless thousands of poor emigrants destined for the 'Land of the free, home of the brave', in search of a better, more prosperous life. Right from the beginning, the American colonies had been a place of refuge for the oppressed minorities of Europe, the victims of religious and racial intolerance as well as the plain poor. They all contributed to

▲ Southampton's New Docks shortly after they were opened in the 1930s, showing many of the liners from all sea routes that operated from the port in those days. Nearest the camera are the *Empress of Britain* and *Europa*.
British Transport Commission

the unique blend of cultures which is America today, and through the heyday of the ocean passenger liner they represented an immense source of revenue.

Ironically, despite their greater numbers, the allocation of space and amenities to the emigrants was grotesquely disproportionate to that enjoyed by their wealthier counterparts, reflecting the very same social inequalities from which they were making their escape. In very round figures, of the total passengers that an Atlantic liner of the Victorian period could accommodate, typically 30% were allocated some 60% or more of the space, and this was the most luxurious and best appointed. Almost the complete reverse was the case for the Steerage passengers. Their cramped quarters were, invariably, low-down in the ship, near the heat and noise of the engines, and were usually laid out as dormitories where eating, sleeping and every other aspect of life was conducted communally, denying even the minimum of privacy.

This remained the state of affairs well into the new century, up to the start of World War 1 — even after engineering and shipbuilding advances permitted the construction of quite massive ocean liners, the like of which had never been seen before. Despite the fact that aboard these ships there were unprecedented amounts of space available for the passengers, it was still generally divided up along traditional lines. It was only after the first great war of the 20th century, as social changes gathered pace, that there was a hint of reapportionment. Facilities previously reserved for the premier classes of passenger were gradually made available in the lower grades of cabin — electric lighting, hot water for washing, heating and *en suite* toilet amenities. Accommodation for the cheaper fares was increasingly provided in private cabins with bunk-type beds.

Some companies, like White Star and the Hamburg Amerika Line, opted for larger vessels of moderate speed, aboard which the emphasis was placed on comfort and luxury. Others, like Cunard and the Norddeutscher Lloyd, pursued speed as their principal marketing tool, and equipped their ships less ostentatiously, though only relatively so. France's flagship operator, the French Line (CGT), carved out a niche somewhere between the two, earning an unrivalled reputation for décor and cuisine.

As with everything else on the Atlantic, the competition for the accolade of fastest crossing, the Blue Riband, ranked above all others. It attracted an interest with the public at large that no other route experienced and it was comparable, in its achievement, with the conquests of the early pioneers and explorers.

The saying goes that 'pride goes before a fall', and in a way so it was for the fortunes of the transatlantic passenger liner. The fact is that nothing can stand in the path of progress — it is an unavoidable dimension of the human condition. Thus it was that, as the ocean passenger liner was completing its twelfth decade, seemingly riding on the crest of a wave, it came up against a form of competition, bred of the desire to make cheaper travel available to all, which it could never defeat. After World War 2, from the low level of recovery as the devastation of six long years of fighting was gradually made good, passenger numbers had increased year on year, far surpassing anything experienced previously. But at the very moment when they reached their highest level ever, they went into steep decline and within 15 years the transatlantic trade had all but disappeared completely.

Every week, for years, up to the late 1960s, the *Isle of Wight County Press* published its column of 'Passenger Liner Movements' listing the arrival and departure times of the liners visiting Great Britain's premier passenger port. Although today passenger ships once more call regularly at Southampton, there were often more ships passing through the Solent in one day back when those old 'Movements' lists were compiled than there are today in a whole month.

Having said that, today there are countless cruise ships operating the various tourist circuits. They are greater in number and many of them are larger and more spacious than the old liners of the Atlantic run. But nothing can compare to those wonderful greyhounds of the Western Ocean whose exploits were legendary and whose names and imagery evoke a romantic era of travel by sea, the like of which will never be seen again. For them, their final 50 years were truly their 'Glory Days'.

David L. Williams
Newport, Isle of Wight
April 2000

1. POSTWAR REVIVAL — THE 1920S

The ravages of World War 1 left the transatlantic passenger business in a parlous, fragmented state and by 1920 it had still barely begun to recover. Many of the ambitious plans hatched in the run-up to war, prior to the outbreak of fighting in the summer of 1914, had been wrecked, as much the victim of the reparations allocations drawn up under the Treaty of Versailles as of U-boat or mine.

White Star's planned trio of giants, already one down through the loss of the *Titanic* in 1912, had been reduced to a single vessel, the *Olympic*, which itself had been a lucky survivor, having had a number of narrow escapes. Albert Ballin's grand project for domination of the North Atlantic run by Hamburg Amerika was another casualty of the war. All three of his massive passenger ships — the largest built up to that time — had survived intact, but the process of compensation dictated by the victorious over the vanquished had carved them up and each of the three vessels was allocated to a different operator. The *Imperator* went to Cunard as the *Berengaria*,

◄◄ French Line ships on the North Atlantic in the 1920s included the *France* of 1912, making what would appear to be excessive speed so close inshore, and…
…the *Paris*, here promoting her Plymouth call in a poster by H. H. Rodmell.
both Author's collection

offsetting the loss of the *Lusitania*. The *Vaterland*, renamed *Leviathan*, joined the youthful United States Lines, after a spell of troop-carrying. The last, and largest, of the trio, the *Bismarck*, was still incomplete at the war's end. She was finished to the account of White Star and rechristened *Majestic*, joining the *Olympic* as a replacement for the *Britannic*, which had been sunk by a mine in 1916 while serving as a hospital ship.

Ironically, France, which had suffered so heavily over the five years of conflict, with much of the fighting on her soil, received nothing from the former German passenger fleet by way of compensation. The French Line (CGT)'s front-line ship, the *France*, had come through unscathed while a slightly larger vessel, the *Paris*, construction of which had begun in 1913 but had been delayed for the duration of the war, was completed at the earliest opportunity, to join her. The *Paris* entered service in June 1921, making her maiden voyage from Le Havre to New York via Plymouth.

The wartime devastation extended beyond the major operators down through all levels of the Atlantic passenger trade. Over the course of the war, no fewer than 54 Atlantic passenger ships had been sunk, comprising a huge 690,000 tons of lost shipping. This had to be made good on the return of peace — indeed, it had to be bettered, for among the social changes that had been accelerated by the war was a growing desire among ordinary citizens to travel abroad, along with an expectation that the quality of their accommodation would benefit from refinements previously reserved for the higher grades of passenger.

The first postwar passenger sailings were most probably made by some of the smaller, less grand passenger liners which made their slower but regular crossings with the minimum of fuss or attention. Inevitably, though, the focus of attention went first to the reintroduction of the premier services to New York and, in particular, the return to commercial schedules of the giant ships — *Aquitania*, *Berengaria*, *Leviathan*, *Majestic*, *Mauretania* and *Olympic* — the 'Big Six' which accounted for the lion's share of the available passenger berths. For one or two of these ships, though, it was a case of only a temporary return to commercial service. As shipyard capacity permitted, their scheduled sailings were once more interrupted as they were taken in hand for

comprehensive refurbishment and conversion to burn oil fuel.

If restoration of the North Atlantic services immediately following World War 1 was primarily influenced by such factors as the distribution of the former German passenger fleet and the speed at which yards could deliver new vessels, so it was that a number of important developments over the next decade were to shape the longer-term postwar transatlantic shipping scene.

Cunard had emerged from the war, despite quite heavy losses of ships, as the dominant operator on the North Atlantic run, rivalled only by White Star. By 1925, with a fleet of 15 ships, the line owned around 20% of the total passenger liners operating on the Western Ocean routes at that time. What is more, these were securing for Cunard a healthy percentage of the available volume of traffic.

American nationals continued to represent the majority of those travelling across the Atlantic, yet a US flag-carrier of proportionate scale, befitting American aspirations, remained conspicuous by its absence. Drawing on the surplus vessels designed and constructed for the United States Shipping Board under the World War 1 emergency shipbuilding programme, an attempt was made to remedy this deficiency by the formation of the United States Mail Line. The company took over eight of the Shipping Board's standard types, all renamed after American Presidents. To these it was intended to add the motley collection of former German vessels, seized in United States ports, as they were released from transportation duties. In the event, only the *America*, previously Hamburg Amerika Line's *Amerika*, and the *George Washington* joined the United States Mail Line before the short-lived enterprise failed.

The US Shipping Board was compelled to step in and take over the operation, creating the original, Government-owned United States Lines. Progressively, the *Republic* (ex-*President Grant*) and *Leviathan* (ex-*Vaterland*) entered service to supplement the fleet of what was, in effect, the national flag-carrier, but it was to be many more years before the United States would truly have the prestigious passenger shipping line to which it aspired.

The early years of the century on the Atlantic had been dominated by the rapid expansion of the International Mercantile Marine Company, an American shipping conglomerate. Now, the 15-year period from 1920 witnessed its gradual dissolution and demise, a process which had a substantial impact on the North Atlantic scene. The IMM story was involved, confused, even convoluted, beginning back in the 1870s when the Red Star Line was formed under the ownership of the International Navigation Company. Established by a group of Philadelphia businessmen, administrative control of the line remained in the United States but the ships were registered in Belgium.

By 1902, under its new operating name, the combine had secured either all or the majority of the share capitals of a large number of North Atlantic shipping lines. As part of its Steamship Amalgamation Plan it had absorbed or acquired control of the American Line, Inman Line, Atlantic Transport Line, Leyland Line, Dominion Line and White Star Line. The ships of these companies operated services to Boston and Philadelphia as well as to New York from Liverpool, London and Antwerp. In addition, close working links were forged with Holland America Line and Norddeutscher Lloyd.

By the mid-1920s the giant concern had reached a critical mass and was fast approaching meltdown. It had already survived liquidation in April 1915 as the result of astute guidance from a receiver appointed by the US Shipping Board, but the deteriorating economic climes in the approach to the Wall Street crash were more than the company could endure. Already, in 1921, the Dominion Line had been absorbed into Leyland Line although its ships retained their original colours. Making its last Atlantic sailings in 1923, the American Line had also effectively suspended operations. Now the IMM's foreign assets were shed one by one in a bid to bolster its finances. White Star Line was sold to the Royal Mail group in 1926, and Red Star gradually ceased trading over the period from 1927 to 1929, its vessels transferred to the Leyland Line, although these too retained the livery of their previous owner. The end for the Atlantic Transport Line came in 1930.

The Leyland Line, the remaining survivor of the IMM's bold attempt to dominate the North Atlantic, was itself destined to continue as a going concern for only another five years.

Quite apart from considerations of décor, the interior layout of new ships entering service from the early 1920s was strongly influenced by two key factors. Firstly, against a backdrop of cut-throat competition, in response to the greater socialisation of ocean travel, provision had to be made for the growing demand for reasonable accommodation at cheaper fares. This trend, manifested both in regular services and on cruise excursions, continued to expand as the decade progressed.

Tourist class, the product of these pressures, was more or less an amalgamation of the bottom end of the old Second class and the top end of the old Third class. It was sometimes

The triple-screw *Belgenland* of Red Star Line. *Philip Rentell collection*

Holland America Line's *Potsdam*. The route for these Dutch ships took them from Rotterdam and Boulogne to New York direct. Calls at Southampton were added later. *Author's collection*

Revealing a once-popular exterior style — two funnels and four masts — Red Star Line's *Lapland*.
Ian Allan Library

The *Regina* served several of the IMM shipping lines as well as other owners. They included Dominion, White Star, Red Star and Holland America Line.
Ian Allan Library

provided in conjunction with a slightly lower-grade Tourist Third, but eventually it replaced all other secondary fare grades.

Like the complicated dealings of the IMM concern, so too the grading of the various classes of accommodation on the transatlantic passenger liners was a confusing and seemingly arbitrary business. The Atlantic Passenger Conference was the body responsible for regulating fare structures according to the types of accommodation each ship offered. Though intended to create the proverbial 'level playing-field' of fair competition, in practice the process seemed to offer considerable opportunity for exploitation and expediency, allowing operators to have their ships graded in such a way that they could secure the most favourable competitive trading position.

The situation was complicated further from May 1921 when the level of immigration into the United States (the quota system) was drastically reduced. The enactment of the Dillingham Immigration Restriction Act confirmed, as suspected, the termination of large-scale immigration into America and with it the redundancy of huge numbers of steerage berths. Efforts were made to convert these obsolete migrant spaces to cater for the growing demand from other categories of passenger. The net effect of these changes was a distinctively different distribution of the cabin spaces and fare structures aboard liners entering service from the mid-1920s onwards, compared with that of 10 or more years earlier.

Yet another change to operating conditions in the wake of World War 1 saw the North Atlantic express mail services from the United Kingdom relocated at Southampton, which thereafter became Britain's premier passenger port. The route from New York to the Channel ports, with a call at Le Havre or Cherbourg and sometimes continuing up the coast of Europe to Bremerhaven, became the main track across the Atlantic. Lesser services continued to operate from Glasgow, Liverpool and London, some making landfall at Boston, others working the Canadian routes to Montreal and Quebec.

Operating the route from Glasgow to New York was the Anchor Line, while the service from Glasgow to Halifax, St John, Montreal and Quebec was maintained by the Donaldson Line, both concerns being closely associated with Cunard. Between them they had lost eight ships during the war at sea

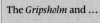

◄ The *Gripsholm* and …

◄ …*Kungsholm*, stylish Swedish America Line motorships introduced on the Atlantic in the 1920s.
both Ian Allan Library

but these were made good by an aggressive rebuilding programme. Six smart, new 16-17,000 tonners were ordered for Anchor, the first, the *Cameronia*, being the first new British liner to be laid down after the cessation of hostilities. In the event only five of the six were delivered to Anchor, the second ship of the first group going instead to Cunard.

Replacements for the war casualties *Letitia* and *Athenia* were built for the Donaldson Line, the new ships taking the names of their predecessors. The second *Athenia* was to become the first passenger ship loss of World War 2 when she was torpedoed within hours of the declaration of war in September 1939.

Already famed for its stylish 'Empress' services, and probably the best known of the lines working the St Lawrence route, was the Canadian Pacific Line, incorporated in Canada but with its ships registered under the Red Ensign. During the war, Canadian Pacific had taken over the Allan Line, a North Atlantic operator with a long heritage extending back to 1854. Between them, the two companies had suffered the next greatest number of wartime casualties after Cunard — nine ships in total. Canadian Pacific rose to the challenge that restoration of these losses represented by launching a rebuilding programme that was rivalled only by that of Cunard. In the 11 years to 1930, the line commissioned no fewer than nine new ships: the *Melita* and *Minnedosa*, the *Montcalm*, *Montrose* and *Montclare*, and culminating in a class of four elegant, 20,000-ton ships — the *Duchess of Atholl*, *Duchess of Bedford*, *Duchess of Richmond* and *Duchess of York*. The 'Duchess' quartet brought a significant upgrade to the calibre of the accommodation on the Canadian services, besides which, apart from the express mail ships, they were a lot faster than their competitors.

Simultaneous with the introduction of these new ships, Canadian Pacific also reinstated its 'Empress' front-line service with the *Empress of Britain* of 1906, *Empress of France* (ex-*Alsatian*) — the only survivor of a pair which were the largest vessels ever to be conceived by the old Allan Line — and the *Empress of Scotland*, a surrendered German liner, originally HAPAG's *Kaiserin Auguste Viktoria*. Later in the decade, the *Empress of Britain* was replaced by the *Empress of Australia*, another former German ship, transferred from the transpacific service.

Norwegian America Line

Twin-Screw Mail and Passenger Service S/S *Stavangerfjord* S/S *Bergensfjord*
NEW YORK · NORWAY · SWEDEN · DENMARK · FINLAND
AND OTHER EUROPEAN COUNTRIES

Elsewhere in Europe, other North Atlantic operators were also picking up the pieces, striving to recover from the legacy of the years of war. Their fortunes had been affected in different ways by the conflict so that, in the process of reinstating their operations, each was confronted by unique problems.

France's champion on the Atlantic run, the French Line had already, before the war, established an enviable reputation for the splendour of its ships' interior appointments, for the quality of the cabin service and, of course, for the gastronomic delights of the best cuisine on the Atlantic. In the early 1920s, the company was pursuing a quite modest rebuilding

Hamburg–Amerika Linie.
Doppelschrauben–Turbinendampfer „Deutschland".

programme which gave no hint of the heights it was to reach within 10 years, and for which it would be long remembered.

Germany was still represented on the North Atlantic routes by the Norddeutscher Lloyd based in Bremen and the Hamburg Amerika Line (HAPAG). Between them they had, in fact, lost only two ships to war action, but the reparations process that followed the Armistice deprived them of the larger part of their surviving serviceable vessels.

After the war, Hamburg Amerika, which had, as already noted, lost its three giant liners, made no attempt to resurrect its North Atlantic service on such a grandiose scale. The

company's first new ships were a quartet of moderately-sized, twin-funnelled steamships which entered service between 1923 and 1927. At the same time, two somewhat smaller cargo-passenger ships, the *Thuringia* and *Westphalia*, were commissioned. Towards the latter half of the decade, two of the line's vessels, which had been transferred first to the Netherlands under a dubious compensation deal and then, when this was challenged, under the American flag to the United American Line, found themselves back in Hamburg Amerika's hands. Of prewar design but completed after the war's end, the *Resolute* and *Reliance* brought enhanced

standards to the Hamburg Amerika service, which until then had been characterised by the rather basic *Albert Ballin*-class ships. Two years later, the smart motor ships, *Milwaukee* and *St Louis*, joined them.

Norddeutscher Lloyd fared a little better than its River Elbe-based counterpart, retaining one of a pair of intermediate steamers, which seems to have escaped the attention of the Reparations Committee simply because its construction was so little advanced. The first of the two liners went to White Star as the *Homeric*, the second ship taking the original name of its former sister, entering service as the *Columbus* in November 1923.

Like Hamburg Amerika, Norddeutscher Lloyd introduced rather small and slow vessels to run alongside the *Columbus*, apparently as part of a strategic refocusing on the less ostentatious sector of the market. These included the *München* and *Stuttgart*, followed by the similar but slightly larger *Berlin*. Inside 10 years, all this was to change, as Norddeutscher Lloyd reasserted itself on a scale that far surpassed its prewar status.

Neutrality had afforded a measure of protection to the Netherlands throughout the war, but it had only been possible to sustain a regular timetable of crossings through U-boat-infested seas with difficulty for, in rough seas and poor visibility, mistakes in the identification of ships were easily

made. As its service had continued more-or-less uninterrupted, Holland America Line's *Nieuw Amsterdam* and *Rotterdam* were among the earliest ships to resume full North Atlantic schedules. However, the company had to endure a long wait for its first new postwar tonnage, the replacement *Statendam*.

The previous ship of that name, completed during the war, had been sunk while serving as a British troopship.

In Scandinavia, following the dissolution of its union with Sweden, creating two separate sovereign states, Norway had established its North Atlantic national flag line in 1913. It was followed in like fashion by Sweden in 1915. These youthful companies, which had not been affected so much by the war, made even more ground in the 1920s with the introduction of splendid new ships. Norwegian America Line took delivery of the *Stavangerfjord* to supplement the earlier *Bergensfjord* whose sister *Kristianafjord* had been wrecked in 1917. As for the Swedish America Line, which operated a service from Gothenburg, the company commissioned the first ships built to its own order, the diesel-engined *Gripsholm* and *Kungsholm*. They entered service in 1925 and 1928.

Last, but not least, Italy's presence on the services to the United States from southern Europe took the form of the vessels of three shipping lines, two operating out of Genoa,

the third, a former Austrian concern, from Trieste. Two pairs of sleek sisters, the *Conte Rosso* and *Conte Verde*, and the larger *Conte Biancamano* and *Conte Grande*, represented Lloyd Sabaudo. Its close rival, the Navigazione Generale Italiana (NGI), initially brought out the twin steamships *Duilio* and *Giulio Cesare* before embarking on even more ambitious plans later in the decade. The contribution of Cosulich was a pair of modern motor ships, the *Saturnia* and *Vulcania*, among the first diesel-engined ships to enter the North Atlantic service.

Before closing this chapter, a brief review of the engineering developments in this period is appropriate, for it was a time of rapid evolution of propulsion systems. At the beginning of the decade, the principal area of change was in the adaptation of the coal-fired furnaces of steamships to allow them to burn oil fuel. Apart from the savings on manpower that coal-to-oil conversions permitted, bunkering also became an easier, cleaner and quicker process.

The steam turbine continued to displace the reciprocating engine as the preferred prime mover for steam-driven vessels, progressing from direct drive through geared propulsion units. Greater power output was progressively derived as new types of boilers permitted the achievement of increased steam pressure.

The decade also saw the arrival of the first ocean passenger ships powered by internal-combustion engines, the *Gripsholm* being the first diesel ship to enter North Atlantic service. She was a hint of what was to come on a much larger scale half a century later. Many advantages were claimed for the internal-combustion engine, among them a better power-to-weight ratio, reduced engine-room crew numbers and a reduction in fuel bunkering spaces.

Now, waiting in the wings, a new generation of giant, express passenger liners was about to enter upon the North Atlantic stage.

Representing Canadian Pacific on the St Lawrence run from Southampton in the 1920s was the *Empress of France* (ex-*Alsatian*).
Ian Allan Library

2. PRIDE OF THE ATLANTIC — THE SHIPS OF STATE

Allegedly, after the end of the Great War, views had been expressed, somewhat illogically, which held that the building of giant express liners, such as the *Aquitania*, *Olympic* and *Titanic*, and the great HAPAG trio, had somehow contributed to the deterioration of relationships between the opposing nations in the recently-ended conflict. It was implied that these huge vessels, as symbols of status and dominance, had fuelled nationalistic rivalry as extensions of the growing military confrontation, contributing indirectly to a growing climate of animosity and fuelling the arms build-up between the great powers. Simple commercial rivalry to secure the cream of the premier traffic did not, it seems, enter into it.

Interestingly, the argument did not also embrace the question of speed supremacy which was more specifically manifested in the challenge for the Atlantic Blue Riband and which was a much more valuable asset for ships which would later be employed in naval support roles. Having eclipsed the four German greyhounds of the early Edwardian years, the *Mauretania* and *Lusitania* had effectively neutralised that particular contest by their huge margin of superiority, some seven years before the outbreak of war. But with Government money behind their genesis and features designed into them to facilitate conversion to auxiliary cruisers, they were, perhaps, a more valid target for these charges.

None of this thinking took commercial practice into account. It ignored the principle of economy of scale and the fact that the size of ocean liners had already been increasing steadily for years. It took no account, either, of the enduring attraction of the largest and fastest ships, which were invariably successful, taking the cream of the passenger trade. It was inevitable, therefore, that before very long — in fact as soon as economic conditions permitted — the race for size would be reactivated.

The catalyst, when it came, was the French Line's *Ile de France*, introduced in June 1927 — not an especially large vessel but one which brought to the Atlantic run a standard of luxury and stylish grandeur in her First-class appointments which surpassed everything that had gone before. For years she was regarded as the most magnificently-decorated liner of her class on the Atlantic, and she regularly carried more First-class passengers than any

◄ Striking evidence of the extreme fire damage sustained by the *Europa* while she was completing at the Blohm & Voss shipyard. The extensive repair work that was required delayed her entry into service. *Blohm & Voss AG*

▲ other ship. At a stroke, her *à la mode* modern décor rendered the interiors of every other ship dated, fussy and old-fashioned. Just as she was not truly a giant — less than 800ft in overall length — so too she was not a speed queen, but she offered other innovations, notably a seaplane catapult, erected on her topmost deck, that could ensure that mails and the odd, really ▶▶ desperate passenger could arrive at their destination in near-record time. The later *Bremen* offered a similar facility.

Prior to the emergence of the *Ile de France*, five of the prewar giants had returned to service with varying degrees of success. The *Aquitania* in consort with the *Berengaria* comprised the most popular pair, carrying almost full passenger complements voyage after voyage. White Star enjoyed a similar level of prosperity with the *Olympic* and *Majestic*, the company benefiting from the publicity of owning the world's largest

ship. Against this, Cunard could still claim to have the fastest ship, in the *Mauretania*. Only the *Leviathan*, the remaining former HAPAG giant, failed to perform profitably on the Atlantic route. Having no comparably-sized vessel to run alongside her, the United States Lines was compelled to operate a single-ship service which spread the schedule over three weeks and made it difficult to attract a loyal patronage from regular travellers. Besides this, she was dogged by higher running-costs and the adverse impact of the Volstead Anti-Alcohol Act, all of which conspired against her and ultimately resulted in her being the first of her class to be retired.

Benefiting from injections of American capital, Nord-deutscher Lloyd had recovered from its low ebb of the early 1920s and was financially stronger than ever before. Against this background, the company elected to make its bid to

Close-up view of the completed *Europa*'s centre section. Her funnels are in their original, squat configuration. They were increased in height later. *Ian Allan Library*

A view along the *Europa*'s boat deck as she made her maiden arrival in the Solent, off Cowes, on 20 March 1930. *Ian Allan Library*

reinstate its Atlantic operation as supreme. In its rakish masterpieces *Bremen* and *Europa* it more than achieved its ambition, if only temporarily, and these ships were not merely contenders for size honours.

Whereas the *Ile de France* had, arguably, the most modern and stylish interior of any ocean liner up to that time, externally she was still reminiscent of an earlier period, having a counter stern and three tall, narrow funnels. By contrast, the German twins exuded modernity in their exterior profile, displaying features which, it could be said, represented a pivotal point in the design evolution of the great Atlantic liners. They had squat, motorship-type funnels and long, low hull lines. A bulbous bow was a distinctive element of their hydrodynamic streamlining, contributing to the reduction of hull resistance below the waterline. They were spacious and stylish, deservingly entitled to recognition as the natural successors to the crown of the Atlantic. They were built for speed, as true thoroughbreds, to win the honours for the fastest crossing times and in this they did not disappoint either. With the *Europa* delayed in the building yard, requiring extensive repairs after a devastating fire and enforced scuttling, it fell to the *Bremen* to take first crack at the Blue Riband when she made her maiden departure on 16 July 1929. After 22 years unrivalled, the *Mauretania*'s long reign as fastest liner on the Atlantic was over. The *Bremen* took the record in both directions. After she finally entered service on 20 March 1930, the *Europa* also notched up record crossings, securing a place for posterity, along with the *Bremen*, on the Atlantic Blue Riband's roll of honour.

The introduction of the *Bremen* and *Europa* provided Norddeutscher Lloyd with an ideal opportunity to upgrade the older *Columbus* and elevate its express service across three ships. She was taken in hand for complete re-engining with geared turbines and, simultaneously, a total refurbishment. When she rejoined the weekly Atlantic mail service, in December 1929, she was 3kt faster and had a drastically restyled appearance, with new broader and shorter funnels resembling those of the *Bremen* and *Europa*. All three liners were marketed together, implying comparable performance, but in truth, despite her thorough overhaul, the *Columbus* struggled to keep up with her larger fleetmates in maintaining the weekly timetable.

These were times of resurgence for Germany but, depressingly, within three years the country was under a National Socialist dictatorship whose aggressive and oppressive intentions were gradually revealed. As the true nature of the régime became apparent, growing numbers of passengers registered their disapproval by shunning the *Bremen* and *Europa*. The pair continued their regular sailings but with reduced passenger complements and diminishing returns. Realistically, without the subsidies they received from the German state, their operation could not have been viably sustained.

For reasons of national prestige, elevating at a stroke the reputation of the Italian merchant marine, the leading Atlantic operators working the 'Sunny Southern Route' from

the Mediterranean to New York commissioned their own giant liners at this time. As serious challengers for size and speed laurels, Navigazione Generale Italiana (NGI) and Lloyd Sabaudo each ordered a single express ship. Whether or not they had plans for consorts we shall never know, for the Italian Government ordered the restructuring of the national passenger shipping lines to rationalise services, with the effect that NGI and Lloyd Sabaudo, along with Cosulich, were joined together to form Italia Flotta Riunite. The two express ships then nearing completion, which had been potential competitors, became fleetmates instead — in effect Mussolini's unique monument to the North Atlantic service. The ships were named *Rex* and *Conte di Savoia* respectively, although the name *Dux* had apparently been considered for the Lloyd Sabaudo contribution to the partnership. The idea was abandoned, perhaps because it was recognised as

The *Conte di Savoia* under construction at Monfalcone. She was launched on 28 October 1931. *Author's collection*

A unique occasion at the Ocean Dock, Southampton, captured on canvas: the trio of former Ballin giants, *Berengaria*, *Leviathan* and *Majestic*, berthed together for the one and only time, on 23 July 1930. *Stephen J. Card*

The *Ile de France*, the liner which re-stimulated the momentum of 'Big Ship' development.
Philip Rentell collection

The *Rex* at speed.
Ian Allan Library

inappropriate, even in Fascist Italy, to associate King Victor Emanuel and 'Il Duce' in this way.

The *Rex* and *Conte di Savoia* were elegant, well-proportioned liners, very similar in appearance, the *Rex* being the larger of the pair and distinguished from the *Conte di Savoia* by the retention of a counter stern. Taking advantage of the warmer temperatures of the more southerly route across the Atlantic, both featured outdoor swimming pools set within lido areas on the open top deck. Their interiors were outstandingly beautiful, the design of their public rooms evoking the grand age of the Italian Baroque, utilising a sumptuous combination of woods, leathers, fabrics and wall coverings.

Only the *Rex* achieved a record time for the Atlantic crossing, during a westbound voyage in 1933. Although she fully deserved her place of honour for the fastest passage up to that time, she held the title all too briefly and she is not, perhaps, thought of as a classic Atlantic greyhound in the way that the *Bremen* and *Europa* are.

The *Conte di Savoia* was distinguished among the giant liners of her era for having three gyro stabilisers installed within her lower hull to suppress movement in rough seas. It was claimed that they restricted rolling in a seaway to a maximum of 2½° either side of upright, even in the most extreme weather conditions.

Probably because they were the only large ships operating to and from the Mediterranean, the *Rex* and *Conte di Savoia* did not noticeably suffer lost patronage as representatives of a Fascist régime in the way that the German liners did.

The introduction of new giants from the early 1930s onwards was not confined to the New York service. In May 1931, Canadian Pacific took delivery of a new *Empress of Britain*, the largest ship ever to operate on the route to Canada. When not employed on regular service work, in the winter months when the St Lawrence was frozen over, she reverted to luxury cruises and she had features designed into her to suit this dual purpose. Compared with the other giant liners

The *Conte di Savoia* departing from one of the Manhattan piers, in a wonderfully evocative 1930s New York port scene.
Moran Towing & Transportation

Masterpiece in close-up — the instantly-recognisable bow and turtle-backed fo'c'sle of the *Normandie* in drydock. *Ian Allan Library*

The spectacular French Line flagship and Atlantic record-breaker *Normandie* at New York. *Author's collection*

▲ of her tonnage, she had a relatively short hull, and this resulted in a higher superstructure, adding to her impressive proportions. More importantly, the determination of her dimensions was consistent with ensuring that she could navigate the Panama Canal when making long-distance pleasure cruises. The *Empress of Britain* was a fast ship, taking the speed record on the Canadian run in 1934 by making a crossing at an average of 25.08kt. Typically British in style, what the *Empress of Britain* lacked in flair externally was more than offset by her luxurious public rooms and other passenger amenities. A planned sister ship never materialised.

▶▶ While the early 1930s are associated with the rivalry between the *Bremen* and *Europa* and the *Rex* and *Conte di Savoia*, the period from 1935 was renowned for the competition between what were probably the two most famous and most glamorous liners ever placed on the transatlantic passenger service. These were French Line's unique *Normandie* and Cunard's *Queen Mary*, the latter being the first half of a planned two-ship weekly express service.

Although the order for the *Queen Mary* was awarded first, the *Normandie* was completed in advance of her British rival, in May 1935. Both ships had experienced delays in construction because of the depressed economic conditions in the wake of the Wall Street crash, but the *Queen Mary* was affected most. Facing the growing threat from the Continental lines, Cunard had taken the bold step to replace its three older ships on the express mail service with just two. The new vessels were euphemistically described as being the smallest possible that would be able to operate profitably while carrying engines sufficiently powerful to provide the required service speed for a four-day crossing — in effect the first ships to exceed 80,000 gross tons. Conceived as a purely Cunard ship to replace the 24-year-old *Berengaria*, the *Queen Mary* was completed for operation by Cunard White Star, the

British Government having insisted on the merger of Britain's two leading Atlantic operators as the condition for advancing a construction loan.

Proud, powerful and British through-and-through, the *Queen Mary* was a wonderful ship, extravagant, opulent and loved by all who worked or sailed aboard her. She singularly lifted the spirits of the British public during a very dark period and encouraged a wider interest in the exploits of passenger ships in a way that no previous liner had ever done. She made her maiden voyage from Southampton on 27 May 1936, a year to the month after the *Normandie* which, having been state-subsidised from the outset, had already settled into her regular schedule.

The *Normandie* had made her entrance on the Atlantic stage like a gorgeous débutante, stunning the audience with her typically French flair. Magnificent in every respect, her graceful lines epitomised the artistic elegance of that period, so that her achievement of high speed semed more an illusion

◀◀ Norddeutscher Lloyd's twin express giants, the *Bremen* and …

▲ …the *Europa*.
both Deutsches Schiffahrtsmuseum

than the result of evident power. Without doubt she was the most beautiful liner ever built for the North Atlantic service. So much praise has been lavished on her, every accolade exhausted in detailing her appointments, that no adjectives are left with which to describe her. Externally she was perfect, pleasing to the eye in every way. From her elegantly-curved clipper bow to her elliptical stern — a one-off — her lines did not convey the impression of the very large ship that she was. In fact, she was the first liner to exceed 1,000ft in length, with a tonnage only marginally smaller than that of the *Queen Mary*. As for her interiors, it is impossible to do them justice in a few lines. Suffice to say that the French Line spared nothing in the creation of their masterpiece. The following extract from publicity material released by the company at the time of her inauguration, describing in detail each of her public spaces, provides a hint of her sumptuous accommodation:

'The First Class Main Hall, 70 feet long by 66 feet wide, and three decks high, is located on Deck B. The after part is separated from the Main Dining Room by monumental doors in gilt bronze, ornamented with medallions on which are pictures of towns in Normandy. The walls of the hall are made of Algerian onyx, set off by hand-wrought copper, which is gilded and oxydised, and by decorations in cast glass. At the forward end of the hall, between Deck B and the Main Deck, there is a large decorative enamel panel.
   'The Main Dining Room on Deck D, measuring 300 feet by 43 feet, is the largest public room on the ship. The walls are composed, for the most part, of decorated and embossed glass panels. There are eight bronze doors opening on to as many small, private dining-rooms.'

From 1935, when the French giant entered service, through to August 1939, the *Normandie* and *Queen Mary* vied with each other to secure speed honours on the Atlantic. As one set a record time so the other would respond by trimming off a small fraction to improve the time for the best passage. In the end the *Queen Mary* accomplished the fastest crossings, retaining the Atlantic Blue Riband unchallenged from 1938 for the next 14 years.

The contest between these supreme ships of state attracted a great deal of publicity, hungrily consumed by enthusiastic ship-lovers. It revealed some interesting facts on the engineering progress that had been made in less than 20 years. For instance, the *Normandie*'s turbo-electric-drive engines (she was only the seventh liner to have such installations) were so efficient that she consumed no more fuel at 29kt than the *Ile de France* burned to achieve 23.5kt. Similarly, the higher steam pressure produced by the *Queen Mary*'s boilers kept her daily fuel consumption at about the same level as that of the old *Berengaria* which was 6kt slower. Perhaps the most surprising statistic, as a contrast between the two giants, was the difference in their maximum rated horsepower to achieve more or less the same maximum speed. Compared to the 210,000shp of the *Queen Mary*, the power output of the *Normandie* was a considerably more efficient 165,000shp, a clear testimony to the reduced resistance made possible by the streamlined qualities of her hull form.

Those who enjoyed the sight of these spectacular liners in that brief interlude could not have realised how short a time they would spend together engaged in friendly rivalry. As the clouds of war began once again to gather, even more plans were on the drawing board for yet bigger and faster giant liners. The *Queen Mary*, as already stated, was only one half of Cunard's planned two-ship weekly express service and her consort, the *Queen Elizabeth*, the intended replacement for the *Aquitania*, was laid

The *Empress of Britain* sailing from Southampton on her maiden voyage on 27 May 1931. Lots of cloche hats and trilbys are on show.
Ian Allan Library

The tennis court located on the *Empress of Britain*'s boat deck was full-size. Her three giant funnels were usually floodlit while in port.
Ian Allan Library

646. LE HAVRE. Le grand Paquebot "NORMANDIE"
de la Compagnie Générale Transatlantique

Longueur 313 m. 75, largeur 36 m. 40,
jauge brute 79.280 tonnes, puissance 160.000 CV,
vitesse 30 nœuds, soit 54 Km. heure,
3.500 passagers.

The marvellous *Normandie*, the most striking ship of her generation. *Author's collection*

A rather faded promotional image for the *Rex* and *Conte di Savoia*, when these Italian ships were on the crest of the Atlantic waves. *William Miller*

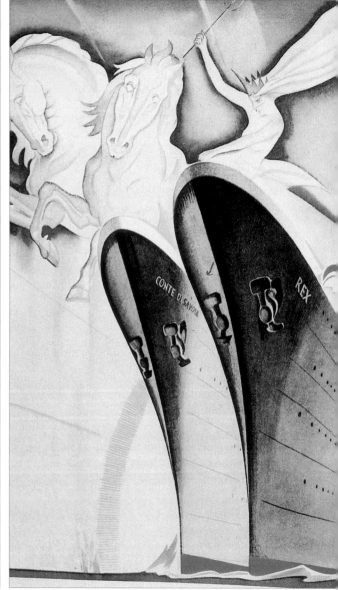

▲ down at the John Brown shipyard on Clydebank in December 1936. She was due for delivery in 1940, the line's centenary year. Meanwhile, the French Line was also hatching plans for a sister for the *Normandie*, for which the name *Bretagne* was
▶ mooted. As for Norddeutscher Lloyd, it too was developing designs for a successor to the *Columbus*. To have been christened *Viktoria*, she would have dwarfed the other new ships under development at over 85,000 gross tons and 1,070ft in overall length. Her massive 300,000shp engine powerplant, driving five propellers, was designed to give her a maximum speed in excess of 36kt, enabling her to wrest the Blue Riband from the *Queen Mary*.

In the event, with the exception of the *Queen Elizabeth*, the outbreak of World War 2 killed off all these projects. In the United States of America, there existed little more than grandiose schemes for monster liners of immense proportions which stood little chance of getting beyond the elaborate artist's impressions presented in press releases. So it was, as the 1930s drew to a close, that the question still remained: where was the much-vaunted giant liner which would fly the Stars and Stripes?

"THE EMPRESS OF BRITAIN READY TO LEAVE SOUTHAMPTON DOCKS FOR CANADA"

SOUTHAMPTON DOCKS
THE GATEWAY TO THE WORLD
Owned and Managed by the Southern Railway.

The *Empress of Britain* preparing to leave Southampton Docks, the 'Gateway to the World'. *Southampton City Cultural Services*

In the 1930s the contrast
between the standards of
accommodation provided for
the poorest and wealthiest
travellers reached its
extreme. The grandeur of the
First-class public rooms in
the premier ships of the day
was so extraordinarily lavish
that it was hard to imagine
that they actually existed
aboard ocean-going vessels.
Here we see the 300ft-long
First-class restaurant aboard
the *Normandie* and one of the
plush lounges of the *Empress
of Britain*. *Ian Allan Library*

3. CABIN SHIPS AND INTERMEDIATE LINERS

The adjective 'intermediate' is a completely unofficial term but, nevertheless, a convenient form of expression by which certain second-rank vessels or passenger liners which fall within the approximate size range of 25,000 to 35,000 gross tons may be categorised — what shipping pundits have long considered to be the ideal size. They were neither as lavishly appointed as the express giants nor, at the other extreme, were they slow or lacking in finery, like some of the very small ships. Generally, they had moderate service speeds and they offered commodious — even, in some cases, very stylish — accommodation. In fact, some of them were their owners' front-line vessels or flagships. Others were conceived as multi-functional units able to cover the express service during periods of overhaul while, at other times in the Atlantic season, they maintained their own, unique schedules. Finally, there were also the pure Cabin ships — a distinct group of ships whose accommodation was innovatively graded to attract a particular class of clientèle.

The already-mentioned *Paris* and *Columbus* are examples of this category, as is the *Belgenland* of Red Star Line. So too is Holland America's handsome *Statendam*, the third of the name, which belatedly entered service in April 1927 after a prolonged construction which had commenced in 1921. These rather similar liners, three conceived prewar, all still reflected earlier design values. They can be considered, therefore, as transitional vessels, taking the 'intermediate' type from the aspidistra and drapery opulence of the Edwardian era to the light veneer, chrome and Bakelite modernism of the Jazz Age. The *Belgenland* fell a casualty of economic forces as the IMM shed its foreign shipping interests. The *Statendam* was an early victim of World War 2.

Two distinctive, new intermediate-sized liners were commissioned by Italy's NGI in the mid-1920s. As demand increased on the Mediterranean service to New York, the operators on this route introduced successively larger vessels, exemplified by Lloyd Sabaudo's *Conte Grande* and *Conte Biancamano*, near-sisters later transferred to other routes, and the Cosulich Line's *Saturnia* and *Vulcania*. These four, already quite large vessels, were capped by NGI's new pair. Smart ships with elegant accommodation, they were identical sisters apart from their propulsion systems. When she entered service, the *Augustus* was the largest motorship in the world. Unusually, she retained steamship-type funnels, making it difficult to distinguish her from the *Roma*, which was powered by geared steam turbines. These popular and well-patronised liners, the precursors to the express giants brought out in the 1930s, reflected Italy's growing aspirations for a stronger position on the sea lanes.

Canadian Pacific launched Cabin class with the *Minnedosa* and her sister, *Melita*. *Ian Allan Library*

The purpose-designed 'Mont' class provided elevated Cabin-class standards on Canadian Pacific's Montreal service. This is the *Montrose*. *Ian Allan Library*

The restyled *Columbus* at speed. *William Miller*

The *Champlain*, French Line's classic Cabin ship. *Frank Braynard*

French Line C.G.T.

S.S. PARIS 34,500 TONS G.

ONE OF A MODERN-ECONOMY TRIO
S.S. CHAMPLAIN · M.S. LAFAYETTE · S.S. PARIS
Extreme Luxury – Speed – Economy
APPLY TO YOUR USUAL TRAVEL AGENT... HIS EXPERT SERVICES COST YOU NOTHING.

SOUTHAMPTON
NEW YORK

The *Columbus* was overhauled and modernised in 1929, to bring her performance and appearance, as far as possible, into line with the *Bremen* and *Europa*.
Deutsches Schiffahrtsmuseum

The *Statendam* was similar in size and style to the *Belgenland*, both being products of the Harland & Wolff shipyard. These elegant ships typified the intermediate transatlantic liners of the early 1920s.
Philip Rentell collection

Prior to World War 1, a number of companies operating on the North Atlantic run had their older three- or four-class ships regraded by the Atlantic Conference in order to give them a more competitive fare structure, to extend their useful lives. The usual practice was to eliminate the old First- and Second-class accommodation and substitute a new fare grade — Cabin-class — which was only slightly more expensive than the former Second. The advantages of this were that quite luxurious standards of accommodation became available at relatively low fares while vast areas of the ship, formerly exclusive to First class, were opened up for the benefit of a greater number of passengers. The vessels that were regraded in this innovative fashion came to be known as Cabin ships.

BRITAIN'S LARGEST
MOTOR VESSEL

M.V. "BRITANNIC" - 27000 TONS

LIVERPOOL & COBH to BOSTON & NEW YORK

WHITE STAR LINE

S.S. Manhattan   United States Lines

The *Paris*, another intermediate liner of pre-World War 1 vintage, seen in a poster promoting her Cabin-ship cousins *Champlain* and *Lafayette*. *Author's collection*

The penultimate White Star liner, the Cabin-class *Britannic*. *Cunard Line*

United States Lines' fortunes started to look up after the entry into service of the *Manhattan* and her sister ship, *Washington*. *Philip Rentell collection*

It did not take discerning ship operators long to realise that there was a considerable demand for this category of fare, which prompted the construction of the first specially-designed Cabin ships. Pioneered by the Canadian Pacific Line, the first purpose-built Cabin ships were the *Missanabie* and *Metagama*, 12,000-gross-ton steamships which had entered service in 1914 and 1915.

After the end of World War 1, with no evident change in the tastes of the travelling public, most companies continued to pursue a Cabin-ship policy for their intermediate or second-rank service. The vessels were typically two-class, offering Cabin and Tourist spaces, or three-class, with the addition of Third-class cabins.

Given that Cabin ships were the product of commercial expediency, it was anticipated that, with their greater attraction to the less affluent, they would fare better than their more luxurious, express counterparts in times of financial stringency.

Three pairs of modern Cabin ships, commissioned in the early 1930s, arrived on the scene at a difficult time for the trans-atlantic trade, seemingly destined to put this hypothesis to the test. By the time the last had entered service, shipping was in deep recession in the wake of the shock waves of the Wall Street crash, and passenger returns were down for all ships on the run.

The first pair to enter service were the French Line ships *Lafayette*, a motorship, and *Champlain*, which was powered by geared turbines. Though outwardly very similar in appearance, the *Lafayette* was the smaller (with one deck fewer) and the shorter of the two. This was very much in keeping with French Line policy which favoured the production of one-off ships. They were outwardly of modern style, each having a single, squat funnel, pear-shaped in section, and a short foremast mounted above the bridge. Apart from being the bigger, the *Champlain* could be distinguished from her consort by the curved cap fitted to her funnel.

Shown in their new Italia livery, the *Roma* and …

…the *Augustus*, largest motor liner in the world at that time. *both Ian Allan Library*

Even by 1930, it had become a natural expectation that successive new CGT liners would herald the introduction of some revolutionary innovation or a radical divergence from convention, either in appearance or décor, and the *Lafayette* and *Champlain* were no exception. While many of their contemporaries still displayed the stiff lines and squared look of an earlier period, the modern profiles of these ships were a portent of the future. They were the first of a generation of stylish CGT vessels that culminated in the *Normandie* in 1935. Other external features included an absence of ventilators and an exaggerated sheer to their hulls. The one concession to the past was the retention of counter sterns. As for their interiors, a contemporary publicity document for the *Lafayette* said it all: 'The design of her public rooms expressed an emphatic "*au revoir*" to the fashions of the past.' The *Champlain* effectively took up where the *Lafayette* left off, a sumptuously-appointed vessel in her own right.

At this point, we pick up the story of the United States Lines which, in 1929, had passed once more into private ownership in a deal which required the new owners to construct a pair of giant express liners to run alongside the *Leviathan*. As the US mail subsidies did not favour ships of this size and as operating conditions in general were unfavourable, no action was taken on the big ships, which would have measured around 45,000 gross tons and 960ft in overall length. Instead, a pair of intermediate Cabin ships was ordered from the New York Shipbuilding Corporation. Even as they were building, they changed hands, however. When the owning company defaulted, by failing to pay its purchase instalments, the Shipping Board was compelled to foreclose and the United States Lines was sold for a second time, in 1931, this time to the remnants of the old IMM. In retrospect, the *Manhattan* and *Washington*, as these liners were christened, could be considered as the phoenix that rose from the funeral pyre of the brief Chapman period of ownership.

For the first time, the United States Lines found itself with a pair of modern passenger vessels which could be operated according to a balanced schedule. They proved to be successful ships, well patronised by American travellers, tastefully and decorously appointed inside and of a generally pleasing exterior design. They measured 24,300 gross tons according

to the system of measurement in force at the time, although remeasurement of the *Washington* after World War 2, at 29,600 gross tons, was a more accurate reflection of their true size. The *Manhattan* and *Washington* were also relatively fast, managing the run from New York to Bremerhaven via Southampton and Cherbourg in six days, at an average speed of 21.5kt.

The third pair of new Cabin ships to be introduced in this period were White Star's *Britannic* and *Georgic*, twin-funnelled motorships which exemplified the Kylsant era of chairmanship of the line, during which there was a special association with Harland & Wolff, the Belfast shipbuilders. They entered service respectively in 1928 and 1932, seeing a combined

▲ United States Lines' *Manhattan* after the height of her funnels had been increased. The *Washington* was virtually identical. *Ian Allan Library*

▼ The gutted hulk of the once-elegant motor liner *Lafayette* is towed away for scrapping near Rotterdam on 12 June 1938. The tugs are, from left, the *Hector*, *Minerva* and *Jeephaven*. *Smit International*

The *Nieuw Amsterdam* and the Statue of Liberty, both wonders of engineering — a poster by Meres.
Author's collection

total of less than 10 years for White Star proper before that company, for all practical purposes, disappeared completely in the merger with Cunard. In that respect, they turned out to be White Star's swansong, being the last vessels to be ordered by that company.

Arguably, the *Britannic* and *Georgic*, like the *Manhattan* and *Washington*, had also been built in preference to a cancelled giant ship. In their case, it was instead of the novel diesel-electric *Oceanic* which, had she been completed, would have been the first Atlantic liner to exceed 1,000ft in length. In the event, she did not proceed beyond the laying of some keel plates.

Regrettably, with their classic motorship lines, the *Britannic* and *Georgic* were not the most attractive liners to be placed on the Atlantic service. Squat and workmanlike in appearance, they were functional and tidy without having quite the flair or stylish-ness of their competitors. Of the three pairs under discussion they were also the slowest. However, of greatest importance, where profitable operation is concerned, was that they were constantly well-booked and consistently paid their way.

Despite the gloom of the early 1930s, the depression in the shipping business gradually lifted as the decade progressed. Politically, international affairs remained unsettled, but on the commercial front there was a sense of optimism that things were getting slowly better. In this climate, a number of Atlantic operators launched projects for new intermediate liners, planning to take advantage of the anticipated upturn in trade.

Holland America Line led the way, ordering a new flagship in 1936, with the prospect of a sister vessel to join her a few years later. The *Statendam* had been running in consort with the 24,150-gross-ton *Rotterdam*, built in 1908. The older vessel was now past her best and it was intended that she should be replaced by the new liner. Christened the *Nieuw Amsterdam* when launched on 10 April 1937, she entered service on 10 May 1938, a most graceful liner and so popular that she soon came to be known as the 'Darling of the Dutch'. She was elegant and modern but in a restrained, intimate way that set her apart from the rather more extravagantly-appointed ships of her day.

The *Nieuw Amsterdam* did not immediately displace the *Rotterdam*, and for two years the three larger Holland America liners maintained a weekly service from Rotterdam to New York, supported by the *Volendam* and *Veendam* which had been commissioned in the early 1920s. Calls were made, out and back, at Boulogne and Southampton.

At this time, Cunard Line ordered a new medium-sized liner to augment the sailings of the *Britannic* and *Georgic*, which had been switched to a London to New York service from April 1935, in a bid to exploit the passenger traffic emanating from the capital. The new ship was given the celebrated name *Mauretania*, reviving an identity which had particularly good associations for Cunard. Besides supporting the London schedules, the new *Mauretania* was also to provide cover for the two 'Queens' on the express service from

Southampton, although the need never actually arose. With this in mind, though, she was given a good turn of speed. Lastly, as if it was necessary to cover all contingencies, it was planned that she should undertake luxury cruises from New York in the winter off-season. She entered service, an excellent ship in all respects and the largest passenger ship up to that time to be built on the River Mersey, on 17 June 1939. With the outbreak of war only a matter of weeks later, all of the plans for the *Mauretania* had to be shelved and she was occupied instead with auxiliary work.

The same outcome afflicted other planned new vessels under construction at this inauspicious time. Capitalising on the strong performances of the *Manhattan* and *Washington*, the United States Lines ordered a third intermediate vessel to replace the ageing *Leviathan*. The new ship, described as being of improved *Manhattan* type, was indeed comparable in size to the earlier pair, but there the similarities ended. With her construction assisted by the United States Government, under the 1936 Merchant Marine Act, and her design entrusted to the famous New York firm of Gibbs & Cox, the *America* was a

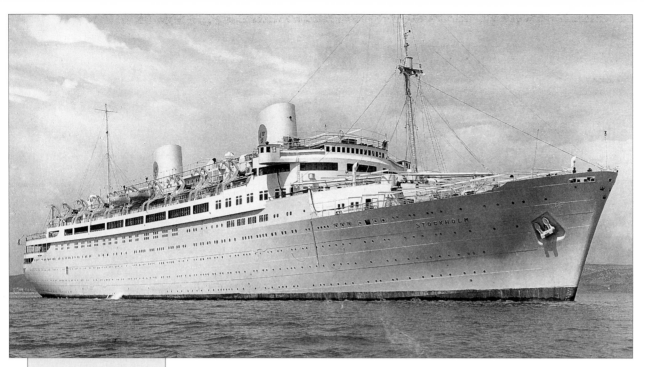

The smart new Swedish
America Line flagship
Stockholm, shown during
trials at Trieste.
CRDA — Author's collection

operating services from Scandinavia and the Baltic, enjoying rapid expansion with good returns from the *Kungsholm* and *Gripsholm*. As an indication of its rapid progress, reflecting confidence in the prospect of continuing growth, the company determined to place an even larger vessel on the route from Gothenburg. Ordered from the Italian shipyard of CRDA, Monfalcone, in 1937, the *Stockholm*, the second of that name, was to be a replacement for the *Drottningholm*, by then a veteran of over 30 years and the oldest ship still working the Atlantic. Incredibly, as a consequence of subsequent events, the *Drottningholm* in fact continued in service for another 15 years, part of it under another flag and two different names.

▲ refreshingly modern liner. From her curved and raked bow to her rounded cruiser stern, and with two squat funnels (of which the foremost was a dummy) topped with 'sampan' fins, she was a really striking ship.

Like the *Manhattan* and *Washington*, the *America* was measured at a rather modest tonnage which did not truly reflect her size, perhaps to secure a more favourable grading under the Atlantic Conference. Later, measurement by other rules gave the *America* the more realistic tonnage of 33,550 gross tons. The hostile situation in Europe from September 1939 prevented her from immediately entering the Atlantic service. Thus from June 1940, when she made her first commercial sailing, she undertook cruises to the Caribbean instead, until taken up for war duties.

By the mid-1930s, the fledgling Swedish America Line was fast reaching maturity as a major player on the North Atlantic. The company had established itself as the principal concern

The *Stockholm* would have been the largest ship ever owned by the Swedish America Line and she constituted a further, major step forward in the quality of the passenger amenities that Swedish America desired to offer. Conceived as a dual-rôle ship, her accommodation layout would have been convertible for cruise excursions. She was to be a luckless ship, though.

Launched on 29 May 1938, the *Stockholm* was swept by a terrible fire on 19 December the same year while she was fitting out, and was completely gutted. All that could be salvaged from her charred remains were her main diesel engines, which had somehow survived intact. This solitary piece of good fortune gave the Swedish America directors a glimmer of hope that the project could be retrieved from the brink of disaster. The construction of an identical vessel was instigated for completion in 1941, two years later than

intended. The replica *Stockholm* progressed to launch even faster than her predecessor, taking to the water on 10 March 1940. By this time, however, World War 2 had broken out and the entrance to the Baltic had been blockaded. The *Stockholm* was never delivered; appropriated by the Italian Government, for conversion into a troopship, she became a war loss.

As late as May 1939, despite the worsening European political scene, the Hamburg Amerika Line launched a bid to re-elevate its position on the Atlantic run to something closer to what it had been a quarter of a century earlier. The company ordered the first of three large liners to replace the unattractive *Albert Ballin*-class ships. Though never officially christened — she was launched without ceremony in September 1940 to clear the slipway — the lead vessel is understood to have been allocated the name *Vaterland*. At 41,000 gross tons and over 800ft in length, these liners would have been at the top end of the notional intermediate category, in itself an amplification of the scale of Hamburg Amerika's upgrade plans. Turbo-electric-drive engines, like those of the *Normandie*, would have given them a 23.5kt service speed, and their accommodation would have provided for 1,322 passengers in three classes. Unfortunately, the *Vaterland* class, along with many other unfulfilled dreams from those years, fell victim to the coming war.

WHITE STAR LINE

SERVICES TO ALL PARTS OF THE WORLD

HEAD OFFICES IN JAMES STREET, LIVERPOOL

From the end of 1933, White Star no longer provided services to all parts of the world — at least, not as an independent company. Featured on the poster is the old *Olympic*. Author's collection

Another Holland America poster. The ship portrayed is either the *Veendam* or *Volendam*. Author's collection

So far we have looked at the new generation of giant express liners and their slightly smaller cousins that entered the Atlantic services in the period between the World Wars. However, just as there are not only Mercedes-Benz and Jaguar cars on the road, but Volkswagen Beetles and Minis too, so the spectrum of Atlantic liner tonnage also includes many smaller, less ostentatious ships among its ranks.

As quality ships in their own right, the smaller vessels worked routes often not supported by the larger, express mail liners. They ranged from the cargo-passenger types, which combined a small quantity of high-grade accommodation, usually in a single class, with their large freight-carrying capacity, to full passenger liners of lesser

▲ tonnage — anything from 10,000 to 20,000 gross tons. They provided passages for all grades of passenger, from exclusive First class to Tourist and Third classes, generally with the less affluent traveller in mind.

▶ Early in the 1920s, White Star had brought out the little Cabin-class ship *Doric*, a liner that was typical of this category of Atlantic passenger vessel, and placed her on the Canadian route from Liverpool. She was more or less a turbine-powered equivalent of the Red Star ships *Pennland* and *Westernland* (all products of the

IMM influence) and she was an excellent ship which served her owners well. A slightly larger consort, the *Laurentic*, which entered service in 1927, was not so successful. For some reason, White Star reverted to reciprocating engines for the main machinery and, in an even more retrograde step, the *Laurentic* remained a coal-burner throughout her life. Until Cunard's takeover ended the White Star régime, she too made regular

HOLLAND-AMERICA LINE
ROTTERDAM - NEW YORK
VIA BOULOGNE SUR MER AND SOUTHAMPTON

sailings on the Liverpool to St Lawrence route. The *Laurentic* did not fit in as comfortably in the post-merger organisation. She was switched to cruising, a short-lived diversion which was abruptly ended after she was involved in a collision off the Skerries in August 1935. Subsequently, apart from occasional trooping voyages for the Government, she was laid up. Less than a month after the *Laurentic*'s mishap, the *Doric* too was involved in a collision. In her case, the damage was so extensive that she was discarded as fit only for scrap. A combination of fate and commercial expedience had eliminated the larger part of the old White Star fleet.

Rather more compact, but further good examples of the smaller Atlantic passenger liner as distinct from the cargo-passenger variety, were the elegant Italian-built, Polish-registered motor liners *Pilsudski* and *Batory* which entered service in 1935 and 1936 respectively.

They were owned by the Gdynia America Shipping Line, a company whose heritage went back to the early part of the century, which had come under Polish control in 1930. The Russian American Line, an East Asiatic subsidiary, was inaugurated in 1906, continuing in operation until World War 1 when, through the force of circumstances, its sailings ceased altogether. Reconstituted in 1921 under the Danish flag as the Baltic American Line, the concern was sold to Polish owners just five years before the first of the new, twin-funnelled motorships was commissioned. Catering primarily for the emigrant trade from eastern Europe, they had cabin spaces graded Tourist and Third-class, and operated between Gdynia, Copenhagen, Halifax and New York on a bi-monthly schedule.

Characterised by high, built-up superstructures on their short hulls, the *Pilsudski* and *Batory* were tidy, comfortably-appointed little ships. They were both popular and successful liners, contributing to a growth in importance of the passenger trade from the Baltic.

The smaller Atlantic liners which combined cargo-carrying, as their primary purpose, with the provision of a relatively

Swedish America Line's *Drottningholm*, something of a veteran by the end of the 1930s. *Philip Rentell collection*

The *Conte Grande*, shown here, and *Conte Biancamano* were sleek Italia liners which worked the Mediterranean route to New York along with their larger fleetmates, *Roma* and *Augustus*. *Ian Allan Library*

Anchor Line's *Cameronia,* which entered the Glasgow to New York service in 1921.
Ian Allan Library

The motor liner *Pilsudski* and her sister *Batory* marked the establishment of a significant presence on the North Atlantic for Poland.
Ian Allan Library

small amount of passenger space were a rather mixed bag, all developed to satisfy the specific needs of niche segments of the Atlantic trade.

The long-established British company Furness Withy had bought the beleaguered Warren Line back in 1912, using the opportunity and the goodwill of the acquisition to implement a cargo passenger service from Liverpool to St John's, Newfoundland, and Halifax, Nova Scotia, a year later. In 1919, the route was extended to include calls at Boston. The passenger spaces on the original ships placed on the service wer strictly limited and begged enhancement in quantity and quality. Thus, in the mid-1920s, the Furness Warren Line, as it was unofficially known, introduced two new, improved steamships, the *Newfoundland* and *Nova Scotia*. They were still rather small, at only 6,800 gross tons with cabin spaces for 105 First-class and 80 Third-class passengers, a modest complement which was invariably fully occupied.

Employment of small cargo-passenger ships on the North Atlantic remained a viable alternative, in spite of the glamour and appeal of crossings aboard the giant express liners. Indeed this sector of the market even expanded between the wars with at least one new operation starting up.

In 1931, American Export Lines, which had originated in 1919 with a cargo-only service, gave the United States a presence on the New York to Mediterranean run when it launched a passenger operation with its first group of so-called 'Four Aces' — the *Excambion*, *Exeter*, *Exochorda* and *Excalibur*. The route took them from New York to Marseilles, Naples, Alexandria, Jaffa, Haifa and Beirut with additional calls, on the return leg, at Piraeus, Livorno and Genoa — a round trip of 46 days' duration, weather and port turn-rounds permitting. At 9,350 gross tons, they offered exclusive one-class accommodation for 125 First-class passengers, later increased to 147. Three of the ships, all of which served as troop transports, did not survive World War 2.

▲ The Anchor-Donaldson liner *Letitia*, a fine example of the many smaller liners that worked the lesser routes across the Atlantic.
Ian Allan Library

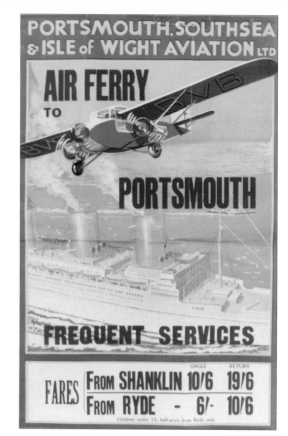

▲ Of comparable size to the American Export quartet were four Holland America cargo-passenger ships originally placed on a service from Rotterdam to Mexico but transferred to the North Atlantic in 1934. Completed between 1921 and 1922, though radically altered later, the *Maasdam*, *Leerdam*, *Edam* and *Spaarndam* worked between Rotterdam and either New York or Baltimore. Berths for 30 Cabin-class and 60 Third-class passengers were provided. Needless to say, this accommo-
► dation, along with the limited public spaces available, was a far cry from the comparative luxury offered in the same grades on the bigger ships. They were slow ships and Holland America aspired to commission better vessels for the cargo-passenger services, even though survivors of the class were retained up to and, as a matter of necessity, beyond the war.

Beginning in 1938, the first of four superior cargo-passenger liners planned for a Rotterdam to New York and Philadelphia service was brought out. This was the 10,700-gross-ton motorship *Noordam*. In fact the four ships were not

quite identical, the first pair, the *Noordam* and her sister ship *Zaandam*, being marginally the faster. There were even differences between these two. Both offered Tourist-only passages, but for only 125 passengers aboard the *Noordam* whereas the *Zaandam* could accommodate 160. The outbreak of hostilities, barely nine months after the *Zaandam* had made her maiden voyage, interfered with Holland America's plans, preventing the completion of the second pair, the *Westerdam* and *Zuiderdam*.

The comings and goings of the various liners of the IMM companies, as these concerns were dissolved, absorbed or integrated, resulted in many changes of ownership.

Furthermore, certain of the combine's ships made early departures for the scrapyard, for example the *Minnetonka* and *Minnewaska*, which had completed only 12 Atlantic seasons.

Only two IMM ships of note remained by the mid-1930s, these being the former Red Star liners *Pennland* and *Westernland*, previously the Dominion Line's *Pittsburgh* and *Regina* respectively. With the disappearance of the final vestiges of the IMM, these vessels, along with the Red Star name and goodwill, were sold to the German operator Arnold Bernstein. They were registered under the German flag while retaining their pre-transfer identities. Their accommodation was completely revamped from March 1935, combining together the three grades previously carried into a single class, all Tourist. The *Pennland* and *Westernland* remained on the Antwerp and Southampton to New York route, making occasional calls at Halifax and Boston. Yet again, this phase of the ships' careers was short-lived for, when the company's owner was arrested during the anti-Semitic purges sweeping

Nazi Germany, this operation, as well as the Bernstein Line proper, was dramatically wound up. The *Pennland* and *Westernland* were sold to Holland America, making a foursome with the nearly equivalent *Volendam* and *Veendam*, although the former pair continued to wear the hull and funnel colours of Red Star.

As already described, of the lines operating from Baltic and Scandinavian ports, the Swedish America Line had overhauled the opposition and, by the closing years of the 1930s, was the dominant company in this region. Not to be completely outdone, its Norwegian counterpart also forged ahead with plans for a new flagship. Though of more modest dimensions than the novel Swedish liner building in Italy, the Norwegian America Line ship was a stylish and graceful vessel, compact yet considerably bigger and more modern than her predecessors. Built in Germany and launched in December 1937 as the *Oslofjord*, unlike her Scandinavian cousin she was actually delivered to her owners. A twin-funnelled motorship,

▲ The *President Roosevelt*, one of two World War 1 US Shipping Board standard ships employed by the United States Lines — for a long period the only tonnage supplementing the schedules of the vastly bigger *Leviathan*. *Alex Duncan*

▼ The *Duchess of Atholl*, lead ship of Canadian Pacific's 'Duchess' quartet. Compare this picture of her with the view of her sister *Duchess of Bedford* on page 64, seen postwar as the *Empress of France*. *Ian Allan Library*

Seen in her original Cosulich
colours, the motor liner
Vulcania provided passages
to New York from Trieste
with her sister *Saturnia*. They
operated what was described
as a 'De Luxe passenger
service to Europe'.
Philip Rentell collection

▲ she could carry 860 passengers in three classes — Cabin,
Tourist and Third. Along with Cunard's *Mauretania* and the
Noordam and *Zaandam*, she was one of the last Atlantic liners
to commence sailings on their intended service before World
War 2. Regrettably, like so many other passenger ships of her
generation, including the *Zaandam*, she did not survive.

By the time war broke out in Europe in September 1939,
there were almost 70 vessels regularly operating sailings
across the Atlantic. Although passenger numbers remained
substantially diminished compared with 20 years earlier, due
largely to the continuing effects of the Depression, as well as
some of the political fallout as increased tensions accompanied
each new confrontation with Germany, the decade of the 1930s
is widely regarded as the period in which the ascendancy of
the transatlantic liner reached its zenith.

This brief span witnessed the arrival of two of the largest
and longest passenger liners ever built, all but one of the
fastest liners ever built, and standards of accommodation
whose luxury and splendour would never be surpassed.
Besides this there were more passenger ships in total on the
run than ever before, with a greater average tonnage. The
Atlantic passenger liner could truly be said, with little fear of
contradiction, to have then been unrivalled as the means of
travelling to and from the New World, with a long and secure
future ahead for it.

Sadly, this glorious era was abruptly ended by World War 2,
during the course of which, and as a consequence of the
necessity to achieve military air superiority with machines of
greater speed and longer range, the ocean liner's ultimate
successor benefited from accelerated development.

5. CALL TO ARMS — NORTH ATLANTIC LINERS ON WAR SERVICE

Like the first global conflict of the 20th century that erupted 25 years earlier, World War 2 had a more profound effect on the transatlantic passenger trade, in its last half century, than almost any other event.

At its end, the service was not just disrupted, as if a temporary interruption had occurred that would be swiftly and simply rectified; the trade had been decimated and it was to take years before it was fully restored. Countless ships had been sunk, some that had survived were no longer fit to resume full passenger-carrying operations, while others had been transferred to new owners under reparations deals as part of the settling of the accounts of war.

To amplify the scale of the devastation, no fewer than three of the five express liners that had secured the accolade of fastest ship on the Atlantic between 1919 and 1939 did not survive. When all of the giant ships commissioned in that 20-year period are taken into consideration, the measure of the havoc is reinforced, for five out of the eight ships of this class were destroyed: *Empress of Britain* (bombed), *Bremen* (accidental fire), *Normandie* (accidental fire), *Rex* (bombed) and *Conte di Savoia* (bombed). Incredibly, the old *Aquitania*, one of the few liners called to serve her country in both wars, had come through unscathed.

The fact was that, for the most part, passenger ships made ideal auxiliaries, as troopships and hospital ships, exploiting their large, ready-to-use accommodation spaces, but also in certain naval support roles, releasing the warships, which otherwise would have been tied up with these duties, for engagement in the combat operations for which they were really intended. All this placed the requisitioned ships in the firing line, constantly exposed to danger. Given the wider extent of the fighting in this second World War, of truly global proportions and involving more adversaries, the hazards were magnified and no sea area could be considered safe. Inevitably, the number of casualties was going to be much higher.

From September 1939, on the outbreak of hostilities, commercial operations were swiftly suspended and the liners were, for the most part, transferred to the custodianship of their respective naval authorities for

conversion into whatever role had been determined for them. Seemingly within weeks, the bright colours of peacetime liveries had been swept away by a tide of grey paint. This was war in earnest, as confirmed by the early sinking of the Donaldson liner *Athenia*, within hours of the declaration of war, at a cost of 112 lives. So it would remain for the next six years.

The North Atlantic ships of Great Britain, Germany, France, Poland and Norway were immediately caught up in the fighting for, while the lack of action on land may have been appropriately described as the 'Phoney War', it was certainly no picnic at sea. Those vessels that had been commandeered for naval auxiliary work were taking up station and experiencing their first encounters with the enemy — uncompromising David versus Goliath clashes in a most inhospitable environment. Others, caught up in foreign parts when the war started, were running for cover, seeking shelter wherever it could be found in neutral or friendly waters.

A flurry of movements of German ships suggested a concerted effort to avoid a repetition of the heavy losses that had been sustained in World War 1 when all that country's liners sheltering in United States ports had been seized. Despite America's declared neutrality for a second time, Germany avoided leaving its passenger liners anywhere within the American sphere of influence. The *Bremen* made her run for home late in 1939, secretively slipping out of New York, empty and without ceremony, running the blockade of waiting British warships. She reached her home port safely after an epic crossing, running silent and blacked-out along a far northern route. The *Columbus*, which was on a luxury cruise to South America when

▲ The troopship *Queen Elizabeth* — the 'Great Grey Ghost', as she was popularly described — made her maiden Atlantic crossing in wartime, sailing alone and taking advantage of her high speed.
World Ship Photo Library

◄ Seen in Valletta Harbour, Malta, the Canadian Pacific liner *Empress of Scotland* (ex-*Empress of Japan*), painted navy grey.
World Ship Photo Library

The USS *Hermitage* (AP54), the former Italia liner *Conte Biancamano*, is shown wearing the United States Navy's protective colouring scheme, Measure 22.
United States National Archives

The *Drottningholm* was engaged for diplomatic service during the war, exchanging prisoners and undertaking other compassionate duties. Her hull had to be distinctively and boldly marked to display her neutral status.
World Ship Photo Library

war started, was not so lucky. Intercepted by British naval units off the coast of Virginia and apparently unwilling to seek refuge in an American port, her crew scuttled her rather than submit to capture.

The main threat to Allied ships early in the war, apart from the obvious and continuing danger posed by U-boats, was the magnetic mine, laid in numbers around the British and French coasts and in the river estuaries leading to deep-water ports. Early victims of these weapons were the *Spaarndam*, in the River Thames, the *Pilsudski* in the River Humber and the *Oslofjord* off the River Tyne. The latter two were operating under the control of the Admiralty after their home countries had been over-run by German forces. The once-beautiful *Champlain* was another mine casualty, sunk off La Pallice on the French Atlantic coast while engaged in the evacuation of civilians and servicemen.

In the early summer of 1940, Germany launched its offensive into Western Europe, striking into the Low Countries and France. In a blatant violation of international law, the neutrality of the Netherlands, which had been recognised 25 years earlier, was completely disregarded. Caught unawares, the vessels of Holland America were trapped in the crossfire as fighting was concentrated in the Rotterdam docks. The *Statendam* was hit repeatedly, set alight and completely destroyed by fire. The *Veendam*, which miraculously escaped serious damage, was seized by the Germans and pressed into service on their account. Her sister *Volendam* came under the control of the British, herself having a lucky escape when she was torpedoed off Bloody Foreland while sailing in a westbound Atlantic convoy with a complement of evacuee children. All were rescued and the *Volendam* was beached, returning to duties after repairs.

As in World War 1, many transatlantic liners were taken over as Armed Merchant Cruisers, relieving the overstretched force of conventional cruisers by carrying out anti-submarine and blockade-breaking patrols and escorting convoys. Notable among the vessels taken over for this role were the Cunard 'A' class ships of the Canadian service (*Alaunia, Andania, Antonia, Ascania, Aurania* and *Ausonia*), the Anchor liners *California, Transylvania* and *Caledonia*, and Canadian Pacific's three Cabin-class 'Mont' ships. Three of these ships were reidentified for naval service. The *Caledonia* commissioned as HMS *Scotstoun*, the *Montcalm* and *Montrose* being renamed HMS *Wolfe* and HMS *Forfar* respectively. World War 1 experience had shown that converted merchant liners, while useful as a short-term expedient, were no match for regular warships and, if attacked, stood little chance. The war at sea from 1939 swiftly demonstrated that the risks inherent in such fundamental inferiority had not diminished, the incidents involving the *Rawalpindi* and the *Jervis Bay* being perhaps the most graphic examples of the consequences of a surface engagement between a heavily-armed battle unit and a thin-plated converted passenger liner. In the event, the *Andania*, the *Forfar* (ex-*Montrose*), the *Transylvania* and the *Scotstoun* (ex-*Caledonia*) were all lost to torpedo attacks within a matter of months of each other, between June and December 1940, while engaged on the Northern Patrol. The surviving vessels were later converted for other duties.

In a conflict of such magnitude, rapidly escalating to engulf nations around the globe — Italy and Greece in 1940, the

United States of America and Japan from 1941, apart from many others — the primary needs of the war effort, to maximise the available forces and provide the right kinds of support as dictated by each campaign, required an unprecedented level of diversification in the utilisation of former passenger liners.

The majority of the Atlantic liners taken up for wartime duties saw service as troop transports, moving huge armies of men to war theatres around the world. Using these ships for this work had its benefits and its disadvantages. The Atlantic liners of that time were among the fastest merchant vessels afloat, permitting the troop convoys to operate at higher speeds than their cargo equivalents. Being capable of average speeds

▲ The transport *West Point* (ex-*America*), arriving at Pier 86, New York, in July 1945 with another large complement of American soldiers returning from Europe. Berthed across the dock is the *Hermitage* (ex-*Conte Biancamano*). *Ian Allan Library*

approaching 30kt, the two Cunard 'Queens' — the *Queen Elizabeth* had joined the *Queen Mary* in March 1940, though not quite in the fashion Cunard had planned for the celebration of its centenary — worked independently of the convoys as this was considered to give them better protection from the submarine wolf-packs. From May 1943, they began the so-called 'GI Shuttle', an essential prerequisite in the build-up to D-Day.

On the downside, conditions below decks were not only cramped but also frequently stifling for the troop complements which travelled aboard these former luxury liners. They had not been designed for work in tropical climates, yet the exigencies of war dictated they operated in regions far from the colder temperatures of the North Atlantic. Besides which, to prevent a catastrophic situation in the event of a torpedo strike, it was usually obligatory to have portholes kept firmly closed throughout the voyage, certainly while passing through those sea areas where the risk was known to be at its greatest. And in those days there was no air conditioning!

Following their brief tour of duty as auxiliary cruisers, the Cunard 'A' ships were converted to Naval Repair Ships. Depot Ship duties awaited the *Montclare* and the HMS *Wolfe* when they were similarly redeployed. Conversion of these ships for their new rôles was extensive, involving substantial structural alterations. When the war ended, the cost to adapt them once more for passenger carrying would have been prohibitively expensive. Thus they were generally regarded as unfit for return to commercial work, working out their lives under the White Ensign.

Equally worthy of mention, Furness Warren's *Newfoundland* was engaged as a hospital ship as was the Italian liner *Saturnia* after the

Americans seized her in the wake of the Italian capitulation in 1943. The *Newfoundland* was lost at Salerno, her prominent Red Cross markings affording no protection from marauding warplanes.

German ships were generally employed as hospital ships or accommodation ships, for the most part locked up in Baltic or North Sea ports. Among them was the Norwegian America Line's *Stavangerfjord*, captured at Oslo in 1940. Later duties were confined to ferry work, conveying military personnel and refugees west along the Baltic coast away from the advancing Red Army.

A feature of the troop movements of World War 2 was participation by these liners in the immense amphibious landings that characterised the Allied assault on the territories occupied by Germany, Italy and Japan. America constructed huge numbers of purpose-designed troop transports specially to support such operations, but former Atlantic passenger liners also joined these invasion fleets and not without cost. As already mentioned, the *Newfoundland* was sunk while engaged in the seaborne landings at Salerno. Two American Export liners, the *Exeter* under the name *Edward Rutledge* and the *Excalibur* as the *Joseph Hewes*, were lost within 24 hours of each other off Casablanca, during the Operation 'Torch' assault on North Africa. A third American Export ship, the *Excambion*, serving as the troopship *John Penn*, was bombed off Guadalcanal in the Pacific in August 1943.

World War 2 cost the Atlantic schedules no fewer than 37 ships sunk and a further 14 which would never again sail as passenger liners on the Western Ocean — of the latter, a very few would make occasional emigrant or troop-carrying crossings, but they were fit for nothing more. Of those that did not survive, a

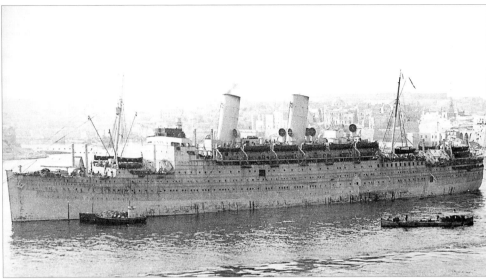

The surrendered *Europa*, still showing the camouflage she was given for the planned invasion of England, Operation 'Sealion'. American occupation forces are reactivating the ship after her capture in the River Weser. *United States National Archives*

Engaged in continuing troop-ferrying work, the *Duchess of Bedford* was photographed at Malta on 14 May 1946. A year later she returned to the Atlantic schedules as the *Empress of France*. *Michael Cassar*

▲ number were lost in some of the worst maritime disasters on record. The *Lancastria* took an unspecified number of occupants down with her — certainly no fewer than 3,000 — when she was hit by bombs off St Nazaire in June 1940. Worse still was the sinking of the *Steuben* off Stolpemünde in early 1945, along with two other German refugee ships. It has been estimated that as many as 15,000 persons in total lost their lives in this catastrophe. In 1942, two British troopships, the *Laconia* and the *Nova Scotia*, were torpedoed and sunk while packed with Italian prisoners of war being transported to England via South Africa. Almost 1,500 of the prisoners aboard the *Laconia* and 650 from the *Nova Scotia* perished in these attacks, in a sense the victims of 'friendly fire'. Another form of prisoner altogether fell victim to air attack in the closing days of the war in Europe. Lying at anchor off Neustadt in the Bay of Lübeck, the Hamburg Amerika liner *Deutschland*, along with the *Cap Arcona*, was holding vast numbers of concentration-camp internees when it came under attack from Allied aircraft. Thousands died. It was a bitter irony that the wretched victims of this bombardment met their fate at the hands of those who, just five days later, would have liberated them.

The employment of Atlantic passenger liners as auxiliaries in World War 2 did not pass without other, less sinister, records being registered. The demands placed on all former liners for the duration of the war were incredible, with vessels routinely denied the engine overhauls that peacetime schedules afforded. Typically, over the course of the war, the larger Atlantic liners clocked up around half a million sea miles — a distance which would not have been covered in double the number of years of commercial service. It was the same for the quantities of passengers carried — in many cases well in excess of what they would have carried at full capacity over their entire peacetime careers. The individual record went to the *Queen Elizabeth*, which, on an eastbound Atlantic voyage in 1944, transported 15,200 American troops — the greatest number of passengers ever carried by a single ship. The outcome, had she been hit by torpedoes, does not bear thinking about.

Such arduous treatment, followed by equally demanding repatriation duties, meant that commercial passenger services across the Atlantic could not be resumed for many months. By necessity these had to wait while the war-weary ships queued to receive long-overdue attention in the shipyards.

6. LEGACY OF WAR — THE CHALLENGE OF RESTORATION

The cessation of hostilities, which offered the prospect of an early resumption of the Atlantic schedules, initially presented as many problems as it resolved. For many of the Atlantic liners, continuing auxiliary work, taking Allied soldiers, and war brides, back to their home countries, kept them from returning to peacetime service. There was a shortage of immediately available tonnage for other reasons too. The many ships that had been sunk had to be replaced but, besides this, there were surviving ships which, for a variety of reasons, could not take their place among the ranks of returning liners.

The *Georgic* had been so badly damaged in a bombing attack at Port Tewfik in 1941 that, although recovered and restored for continuing troop duties, she was in no fit state to resume commercial passenger-carrying operations. A similar fate befell United States Lines' *Manhattan*, which had suffered an on-board fire in mid-Atlantic while sailing in convoy. Towed first to Halifax and then to Boston, she was nothing more than an empty, buckled shell. Like the Tin Man in *The Wizard of Oz* (a popular movie showing in cinemas at the time) she had lost her heart. Wartime needs demanded her reconstruction too; otherwise she and the *Georgic* would surely have gone for scrap. Extensive as the *Manhattan*'s restoration was, though, she would never again cross the Atlantic with civilian passengers.

Germany's passenger fleet had been decimated. Apart from those vessels that had been sunk, the remainder were taken by the Allies and allocated as compensation for the losses sustained over the course of the war. After the briefest tours of duty, ferrying GIs under the United States flag, the *Europa* went to the French Line as a rather inadequate substitute for the *Normandie*. She re-emerged as the *Liberté* — a very appropriate name given the wartime experience of the French — after the most comprehensive rebuilding.

The Russians seized those damaged German liners that had been abandoned along the Baltic coast in varying states of disrepair and had them rebuilt in East Germany for their services on the Black Sea and in the Far East. The old *Hansa* became the *Sovietski Soyuz*, while the *Berlin* returned to

passenger duties after an 11-year refurbishment as the *Admiral Nahimov*. The *Hansa*'s former sister ship, the *Hamburg*, was turned into a fish-factory ship, becoming the flagship of the Soviet Union's deep-sea fishing fleet.

One of the greatest casualties of the war was not a liner but a long-standing North Atlantic operator. The Anchor Line had effectively severed its connection with the Atlantic scene back in 1940. Having lost all its remaining ships during the war, the final Atlantic sailing of this famous line, which had served the route since 1856, was made by the *Cameronia* when she departed New York for the Clyde on 4 November 1940. Upon her arrival in the United Kingdom she was converted into a troopship. She remained in Government hands after the war, as the *Empire Clyde*, until scrapped in 1958.

Despite the difficulties operators were experiencing, it was considered important to reinstate services across the Atlantic at the earliest opportunity. As powerful symbols of a return to normality it was felt that the reappearance of ocean liners in their commercial colours, many of them well remembered, would have a positive effect on morale in the austere, anti-climactic years following the war.

▲ The *Conte Biancamano* as rebuilt postwar. Compare this picture with the view of the *Conte Grande* on page 45. Italia Line

It wasn't exactly a race to see which ship could make the first departure but, inevitably, there was interest in — even a degree of recognition for — the vessel that made the inaugural postwar commercial crossing. In the event, the honours went to Norwegian America's *Stavangerfjord*, which resumed sailings in August 1945 some 11 months ahead of Holland America Line's *Westerdam*, which cleared Rotterdam for New York on 8 July 1946; the latter was followed soon after by her near-sister *Noordam*. Hard on their heels came the *Queen Elizabeth*, whose refurbishment had been given priority, on 25 October 1946 and the *America* on 14 November 1946, the former westbound, the latter heading east. The *Westerdam, Queen Elizabeth* and *America* were all making their maiden commercial voyages.

Cunard was in a position to dominate the North Atlantic trade, having had the singular good fortune of having both of its big ships come through the war unscathed. The company sought to take advantage of its propitious situation, with the full encouragement of the British Government, by getting all its major fleet units back in service ahead of the competition; by the end of 1948 it had six ships back on the run. Of greatest significance, the *Queen Mary* made her first peacetime sailing on 31 July 1947, joining the *Queen Elizabeth* and finally

permitting the implementation of Cunard's coveted two-ship weekly express service. The *Mauretania* had returned to passenger service two months earlier, and in May 1948 the *Britannic* cleared Liverpool on her first postwar departure. To these prewar ships were added the new cargo-passenger liners *Media* and *Parthia* in August 1947 and April 1948.

Most of the established operators managed to get at least one of their ships back into service during 1947. Canadian Pacific had few ships left to call on, so severe had the company's wartime losses been. The two remaining 'Duchess' liners were upgraded and pressed into service as the *Empress of Canada* and *Empress of France*, the first-named making her début sailing in July 1947. The former Pacific liner *Empress of Japan*, which had been prudently renamed *Empress of Scotland* in 1942, joined the older pair on the Montreal route in 1950.

Having served magnificently in the war and after returning Queen Wilhelmina and her Government to the Netherlands,

the pride of the Dutch fleet, the *Nieuw Amsterdam*, re-established the premier service from Rotterdam from October 1947. The *Veendam* and *Volendam* preceded her, earlier in the same year.

The Scandinavian lines had enjoyed mixed fortunes over the years of conflict. Taking advantage of their condition of neutrality, Swedish America's *Gripsholm* and *Drottningholm* had been engaged for a diplomatic operation, ferrying exchanged prisoners and other diplomatically-immune persons under the auspices of the International Red Cross. In complete contrast, the *Kungsholm* had been purchased by the Americans and spent the same years as a troopship under the name *John Ericson*. In 1946 the *Drottningholm* briefly reopened the Swedish America service from Gothenburg before being sold on to new owners; the *Gripsholm* joined her soon after. The *Kungsholm* was repurchased from the United States Government but, having suffered a serious fire while refitting, she was immediately resold.

American Export Line's *Independence* and *Constitution* were a mixture of old and new, contemporary and traditional. They elevated the standard of United States flag-carriers on the Mediterranean run. *Constitution* is shown here, *Richard de Kerbrech collection*

United States Lines' *America*, postwar. She clocked up 18 years on the route from New York to Bremerhaven before she was sold on for further service in 1964. *Roger Sherlock*

Greek Line's first new ship was the *Olympia*, completed at the Glasgow yard of Alexander Stephen & Sons in 1953. *Ian Allan Library*

▲   The ships of two apparently new companies were evident
in the Atlantic passenger trade soon after the end of the war,
these being the Greek Line and the Home Lines, the latter
being the new owner of Swedish America's *Drottningholm* and
Kungsholm. In fact, the Greek Line was not a new entrant into
the Atlantic business, having commenced Atlantic passenger
sailings from Piraeus in April 1939 and maintained them, all
too briefly, with the *Nea Hellas*, the former Anchor liner
Tuscania. Sailings had continued until 1941 when, following
the Axis' invasion of the Greek mainland, dragging that
country into the war, they were forcibly suspended. The
service was reinstated with the *Katoomba*, a vessel previously
employed in the Australian coastal trade. The *Nea Hellas*,
which had served as a troopship, returned in 1947. Other
second-hand vessels were commissioned to complement the
pair, rapidly building up the operation.

   Home Lines was a completely new outfit, registered in
Panama and originally destined to run passenger services to
Latin American ports from the Mediterranean. As it turned
out, Germany was destined not to make a reappearance on
the Atlantic run until 1955, so the company switched to the

North Atlantic run instead to exploit this absence and capture
a large slice of the booming German emigrant traffic. The Home
Lines fleet comprised four quality vessels, even though they
were, for the most part, mature in years. Among them were
the *Italia*, previously Swedish America's *Kungsholm*, and the
Atlantic, which had started life on Matson's route from San
Francisco to Hawaii as the *Matsonia*. The *Drottningholm* and the
old *Bergensfjord*, as the *Brasil* and *Argentina* respectively, made
up the original quartet of ships that Home owned by 1950.

   Also seeking German emigrant custom, Greek Line moved
its second-hand ships to Hamburg and established new
services from there to both New York and Canada. Both Greek
Line and Home Lines subsequently took delivery of improved
vessels as their operations strengthened.

   The services to New York from the Mediterranean were
rapidly reinstated by Italia and American Export. Italia
recommenced its sailings with the *Saturnia* and *Vulcania*
which had been returned to the company by the Americans
after the war. The pair was supplemented with the restyled
Conte Grande and *Conte Biancamano* from 1950 but working in
the summer months only.

◄ The reconstructed *Conte Biancamano* making her final departure from New York. *Ian Shiffman*

► The *Batory* of Polish Ocean Lines— a picture taken of her at Cape Town at the end of her career, en route to the breakers' yard. *Ian Shiffman*

▼ Zim Israel Line's *Jerusalem*, formerly the *Bergensfjord* of Norwegian America Line, was 40 years old when she joined the infant Israeli company; she survived for a further six years. The picture was taken at New York on 31 August 1955. *Ian Shiffman*

As was the case for Canadian Pacific, Swedish America and Norwegian America, these restorative actions were all stopgap measures as operators bought time while their plans for replacement vessels were under development.

A completely new 'Four Aces' quartet was introduced by American Export in 1948 to replace the original ships, three of which had been sunk while the fourth had remained with the US Government engaged in military transportation work. These replacement vessels were all converted, war-built standard ships, taking the names of their predecessors. American Export's cargo-passenger service was boosted with the addition of the larger *La Guardia*, a chartered former 'P2' standard-type naval transport. Able to carry 609 passengers in First and Tourist classes, the *La Guardia* was a hint of things to come, presaging the arrival of the completely new *Constitution* and *Independence* in the early 1950s.

Perhaps the most striking absence from the Atlantic schedules for a long spell after World War 2 was that of the French Line. Having lost its flagship, by far the most glamorous liner ever to grace the Atlantic crossing, the line was dogged by more misfortune in the war's aftermath. The rebuilding *Liberté* was holed during a storm at Le Havre when she struck the still-uncleared wreck of the *Paris*, which had been destroyed by fire back in 1938. Settling on an even keel, luckily she was none the worse for this second enforced immersion of her career, but her reconstruction was seriously delayed, disrupting the French Line's plans for the recommencement of operations. It had already committed to an ambitious and extensive refurbishment of the *Ile de France*; though she presented a somewhat modernised appearance on her return, along with the prospects of a renewed acquaintance with the French Line's legendary food and service, she did not resume passenger sailings until July 1949. For three years, therefore, French Line's only presence on the Atlantic was the *De Grasse*, which worked the route from July

1947, following a full refit, to 1952, when she was transferred to the West Indies route as initially intended. The *De Grasse* had been sunk in the war as a blockship at Bordeaux, and restoration, in her case too, had to wait until after her hull had been raised.

A feature of the Atlantic trade in the wake of the war was a blatant manifestation of the changing political allegiances to which some ships fell victim. The *Batory* — the remaining half of Gdynia America's prewar motorship pair — for one was refused berthing rights at New York as the undesirable representative of an Eastern block régime. Maintaining the schedules with the *Batory*, in place of the lost *Pilsudski*, was the *Sobieski*, herself the remaining survivor of another pair of liners;

she too was denied entry into the port. Gdynia America had no choice but to switch the two ships to an Indian service, prior to the early disposal of the *Sobieski* to the Soviet Union. The company restyled itself as Polish Ocean Lines in recognition of the wider sphere of its operations but, in the late 1950s, the *Batory* returned again to the Atlantic, then making crossings on the St Lawrence route.

Apart from the new ships *Media* and *Parthia*, already mentioned, there were other débutantes in this immediate postwar period — a number that grew as the output of new tonnage from the shipyards began to accelerate. Vickers, on the River Tyne, delivered a new *Nova Scotia* and *Newfoundland* to the Furness Warren Line in 1947 and 1948, replacing the

▲ Another view of the *Batory* painted in the grey hull colour adopted by Gdynia America Line in the 1950s. *Alex Duncan*

The *Empress of France*
(ex-*Duchess of Bedford*).
Ian Shiffman

The Atlantic emigrant carrier
Groote Beer, one of three
converted Victory ships
operated by the Netherlands
Government. *Ian Shiffman*

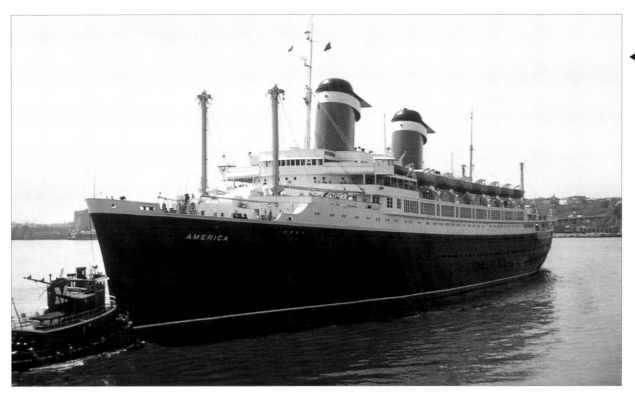

Being handled by tugs of the Moran fleet at New York, the *America*, looking quite splendid in her United States Lines colours. *Ian Shiffman*

After a major reconstruction between April 1947 and July 1949, the *Ile de France* emerged extensively restyled, with one funnel fewer. She is berthed at her home port, Le Havre. *F. Trehet*

▲ two ships of these names that had been lost. Slightly larger
than the earlier pair, they could accommodate 155 passengers
in two classes.

Swedish America Line finally got its *Stockholm* in 1948 but,
though striking in appearance, she was a pale shadow of the
more grandiose ships that the concern had been hoping to
commission a decade earlier. She was low and sleek with
yacht-like proportions, and her hull was reinforced for
operation through ice — a feature which was to have a major
bearing on an incident in July 1956 (see Chapter 8). However,
at just 12,000 gross tons, she was able to carry only 395
passengers maximum — the majority in Tourist class.

The ship of the year in 1949 was undoubtedly Cunard's new
Caronia, an impressive and innovative liner which, with a
single huge funnel and painted in colours that were a
complete departure from anything seen previously, could not
be mistaken for any other. She was swiftly dubbed the 'Green
Goddess'. She was a dual-rôle vessel, intended primarily for
dollar-earning luxury cruises with occasional Atlantic sailing
out-of-season in support of the *Mauretania*.

The same year witnessed the arrival of Norwegian America
Line's first new postwar ship, the *Oslofjord*, which again
replaced a war casualty of the same name. Though somewhat
smaller than the *Caronia*, she was nevertheless another
graceful, modern-styled ship with a single curved and raked
funnel, an elegant clipper bow and smoothed and rounded
contours. She set the style for a series of subsequent liners
introduced to the Oslo service.

With the dawning of the 1950s, the North Atlantic
passenger trade was largely back in its stride. It was set to
enter a phase in which, as the momentum of restoration
quickened, it would be elevated to unprecedented heights.
This was to be the era which would witness more passengers
than ever before crossing the ocean by ship, defying the
challenge of the aeroplane. To carry these multitudes of
passengers there would be a glut of new and reconditioned
ships brought into service — everything from small emigrant
carriers to giant, luxury express mail ships.

The rather basic character of the Dutch trio of emigrant ships is clearly revealed in this view of the *Waterman*. *Alex Duncan*

Holland America opened its postwar account with the first sailing of the *Westerdam*. *Alex Duncan*

The *Empress of Scotland* departing Liverpool on another Atlantic voyage on 29 July 1957. *Ian Shiffman*

One of the postwar 'Four Aces' quartet, the *Excalibur*. *Ian Shiffman*

7. THE FINAL DECADES — A NEW RACE FOR SUPREMACY

With the return of peace, after victory had been secured in Europe, only four of the nine prewar giants (including the *Queen Elizabeth*) remained in existence. Of these, two were now 20 or so years old. Postwar building constraints — essentially a lack of shipyard capacity — dictated that they should receive comprehensive upgrades to extend their lives for at least another 10 years rather than be replaced at that time.

The principal operators, with the exception of Cunard, which had the two 'Queens', were clearly biding their time, seeking initially to consolidate their resources while waiting to see how things would unfold. Major decisions regarding capital investments of the size that giant ships called for required a sound business framework for their gestation. At that time, there was no reason to believe that the North

Atlantic passenger business would not now experience the growth in traffic volumes that had been anticipated back in the late 1930s before international tensions erupted into open conflict and brought everything to a temporary halt. True, in the early 1950s, the Cold War was at its frostiest and the Korean War threatened to escalate into a wider affair but, on the plus side, the economies of the West were vibrant and social emancipation had created a growing population of would-be travellers.

The United States had still not fulfilled its ambition to place its own giant passenger liner on the Atlantic run but the opportunity finally arose when, in 1949, the United States Government indicated a willingness to subsidise the construction and operation of such a ship. A prerequisite was

◀ The *United States* completing at Newport News with her consort *America*, presumably at the shipyard during a refit.
Ian Allan Library

that the vessel should be available for auxiliary duties in national emergencies, as a high-speed troopship, and the design of the ship, which was actually built to the order and specification of the United States Navy, took this into account. In effect, this meant that fundamental financial considerations that were obligatory to just about every other ship-owner could be disregarded, or at least minimised, where this new United States Lines liner was concerned.

In practical terms this meant that the ship could be fitted with a disproportionately large powerplant which, if fitted in any other ship, would have meant unaffordable running costs. It would also mean that the ultimate challenge for the Atlantic Blue Riband was seriously on the cards. Other innovations included the extensive use of aluminium in the ship's upperworks and a near-absence of inflammable materials. Watertight sub-division was, as might be expected, to the

standard typically applied to warships. The principal dimensions were restricted to the maximum which would still permit the vessel to transit the Panama Canal.

The result of all this was the magnificent *United States*. Like the *America* before her, she was built in a shipyard that was becoming increasingly a specialist naval constructor, taking shape alongside aircraft carriers and other warships. Assembled on an even keel in a graving dock, the *United States* was floated out rather than launched into the water — yet another departure from normal practice.

On 3 July 1952, resplendent in her United States Lines livery, her massive crimson, white and blue funnels particularly striking, the *United States* made her maiden departure from New York. Only on this inaugural crossing — it was all that was needed — was she really opened up to reveal the full extent of her speed credentials. In so doing, she smashed the

Queen Mary's record crossing-time by the biggest margin of improvement in the history of the Atlantic Blue Riband. Her eastbound crossing was completed in three days, 10 hours and 40 minutes at the average speed of 35.39kt; on the return voyage she covered the same measured distance in three days, 12 hours and 12 minutes at 34.51kt average speed — records which have yet, almost 50 years later, to be broken. Her service speed was subsequently adjusted down to allow, as near as possible, a balanced schedule working alongside her consort, the *America*. That said, over the 130 Atlantic passages she completed in her first three years of service, the *United States* averaged 30.63kt, an incredibly high level of consistent performance.

The *United States*' long, low profile in many respects hinted of the earlier *America* but, in contrast, she was every bit a racer, a true thoroughbred and, in satisfaction of national aspirations, she was a flag-carrier of which the United States of America could be justifiably proud. Her interiors were stylish, very modern and, while not on a par with the opulent décor of the prewar giants, elegant and tasteful in the mode of the grand metropolitan hotels of that era. If the genesis of the *United States* was somewhat unorthodox, nevertheless she reflected the growing confidence that typified the North Atlantic trade of the 1950s, and in those boom years she acted as a catalyst for the introduction of more transatlantic giants.

The *Liberté* in the eastern Solent, off the Motherbank, prior to having extentions added to her funnels.
Phil Fricker

French Line's *Liberté* in a typically artistic poster designed by Edouard Collin.
Author's collection

▲ Despite the lateness of the company's return to the transatlantic premier service, the French Line had fully re-established its operations by the mid-1950s, and a committed patronage was once more ensuring that the *Ile de France* and *Liberté* regularly sailed with near-full complements. Reconstruction and a change of colour had done a lot to hide the original identity of the *Liberté*. Heightening of her funnels in 1954 gave her an even more distinctive appearance, confirming her as a French Line ship, and few, from that time, continued to think of her as the former *Europa*.

With five giants back on the run and traffic volumes healthier than they had ever been, the North Atlantic passenger service was close to its peak, and, though things would never again be quite as glamorous as they had been in the 1930s, marketeers made every effort to conjure up the ambience of the past. Celebrating the ocean liner's elegant status in the popular imagination, several of the prewar giants had been featured in cinema productions, for example the *Rex* in *Dodsworth* and the *Normandie* in *Paris to New York*. Emulating this unique form of stardom, as if to reinforce the resurgence of the swank and

C^{IE} G^{LE} TRANSATLANTIQUE
French Line

"LIBERTÉ"
LE HAVRE · SOUTHAMPTON · NEW·YORK

exclusive grandeur of the top liners, the *Liberté* was now featured in *The French Line*, co-starring with Jane Russell and Marilyn Monroe, while the *United States* provided the setting for an equally banal screenplay filmed as *Bon Voyage*. It was all but a short interlude in a carefree, optimistic decade that veiled the ominous reality waiting in the wings.

As the 1950s progressed, the *Ile de France* and the *Liberté* edged nearer to 30 years of age, and the need for replacements was becoming imperative. In truth, a new ship would be a replacement for the *Normandie*, but while the French Line conceived a truly marvellous ship she was still not in quite the same league as the earlier vessel whose luxury has never been equalled. Slightly longer overall, at 1,035ft, but with a smaller tonnage, at 66,348 gross tons, she exhibited through the graceful lines of her hull and upperworks some of the design features of the *Normandie*. Dominating her superstructure were two streamlined funnels with fins extending outboard to help disperse exhaust gases. Launched as the *France* on

11 May 1960, she made her début on the Atlantic run on 3 February 1962.

The *France* was one of the last large liners to be designed and constructed specifically for the North Atlantic scheduled passenger service, unfortunately arriving on the scene after that trade had peaked and was already in decline. She depended on subsidies from the French Government, without which she would never have paid her way. Indeed, when these were withdrawn, her brief career as a transatlantic liner was brought to an abrupt and premature end.

Unlike the *United States*, the *France* was not intended to compete for Blue Riband honours, even though her maximum

The *Liberté* underway — a photograph taken after her funnels were heightened.
Ian Shiffman

The *United States*, the fastest liner ever to cross the Atlantic, in a classic view of her flat-out at high speed. *Ian Allan Library*

speed was an impressive 35.2kt. However, this still compared unfavourably with the American ship's top speed, which, as revealed later, when the information was declassified, was a phenomenal 38.3kt — almost 45mph.

Inevitably, comparisons were made between the interiors of the *France* and *Normandie*, an exercise that was both inappropriate and rather pointless — they were different ships for different eras. As a measure of the difference in *raison d'être* of the two liners, the *France* was a two-class ship with 1,637 of her 2,044 passengers accommodated in Tourist class. In contrast, the *Normandie*, a three-class ship, had the greatest percentage of her passenger complement in First class — 848 of the 1,972 total passengers she could carry. Of the remainder, 670 were in Tourist class and 454, the smallest element, in Third class.

The *France* was, in fact, beautifully appointed, although in a style that was not to everyone's taste. Her passengers, those in First class in particular, could enjoy a crossing in luxurious and comfortable surroundings. Despite this, the *France*'s décor was criticised as vulgar and tasteless, lacking that quintessential finesse and refinement routinely associated with the most fashionable operator on the Atlantic.

The emergence of the *France* acted as a trigger for renewed discussion regarding a new Cunard giant. By this time the *Queen Mary* was over a quarter-century old. By 1968, only six years later, both 'Queens' would have been afloat for more than 30 years. A ship very similar in concept to the *France* and dubbed the 'Q3' was contemplated, but, influenced by the drastic downward trend in passenger returns over the three or so years since the *France*'s inception, Cunard's projected ship was first postponed and then cancelled altogether. When Cunard did take delivery of its replacement for the two older 'Queens', the *Queen Elizabeth 2*, she was an altogether different ship. Even then, she constituted something of an experimental vessel for which there was no precedent, destined to sail in uncharted waters.

The curtain finally came down on the career of the *Ile de France* in October 1958, long before the *France* had even been completed. Barely two months before the new liner's entry into service, the *Liberté* too was withdrawn. She arrived at the scrapyard in La Spezia only a matter of days after the *France* had commenced her maiden voyage. It really was a case of one for the price of two. The number of giants had fallen once again to just four — one American, one French and two British.

Incredible as it now seems, given the uncertain background, the Italia Line chose this moment to press ahead with plans for not one but two large new liners for the southern route to New York. Apart from the *Bremen* and *Europa*, they were to be the only true giant sister ships to be completed for the Atlantic run. Italia had contented itself until then with a succession of smart, intermediate-sized ships introduced from the early 1950s as it launched its postwar rebuilding programme. It came as something of a surprise when the *Michelangelo* and *Raffaello* were commissioned in 1965, even though they had undergone a protracted construction with numerous design changes. Naturally enough, they were a reminder of the prewar duo *Rex*

and *Conte di Savoia* but, unlike their predecessors, they were
sleek, white-hulled liners with beautiful lines dominated by
novel lattice-encased funnel structures. At just under 46,000
gross tons they were the smallest of the postwar giants and,
measuring 906ft in overall length, the shortest too.

In consort with the *Leonardo da Vinci* and the *Cristoforo
Colombo*, the new Italian ships maintained the run from
Genoa to New York — the *Michelangelo* from 12 May 1965 and
the *Raffaello* from 25 July the same year — offering voyagers
who were making crossings to and from the Mediterranean
the spaciousness and quality of accommodation which, since
1945, had been restricted to passages out of north European
ports. Financed by the state, they were, no doubt, impractical
vessels for their time and, like the *France*, enjoyed the shortest

of careers on the run for which they had been conceived.
Identical in all respects, apart from their interior decoration,
the *Michelangelo* and *Raffaello* were the giant scheduled liner's
swansong. All the large ships built in the future which
exceeded their dimensions were either of the dual-rôle type
or were dedicated, purpose-designed cruise ships.

For a brief time, the *Michelangelo* and *Raffaello*, along with
the *France* and the later *Queen Elizabeth 2*, held out the hope
that the ocean liner trade could somehow resist the insidious
erosion of the passenger air transport's challenge. In the event
it was a forlorn hope, for these four ships, besides the *United
States* and the earlier 'Queens', were neither able to sustain
their own existence nor fully restore the glamorous image of
the transatlantic tradition.

The Italia liner *Michelangelo* running trials, showing off her classically sleek hull-lines. *Italia Line*

The *Michelangelo* departing Genoa in December 1968. *Ian Shiffman*

The *Michelangelo* again (on the right), with her sister *Raffaello*, berthed together at Genoa. Their most distinctive feature was their novel funnel structures. *Italia Line*

The *France* provided advertising executives with enormous creative opportunities, as these poster and advertisement designs reveal. *both Author's collection*

Portrayed against a dramatically-stylised Manhattan setting, a poster advertising the new *United States*. *Author's collection*

8. THE FINAL DECADES — THE TRANSATLANTIC RUN AT ITS PEAK

As the 1950s progressed and the momentum of regeneration continued to accelerate, the number of passenger liners operating regular services across the Atlantic increased to almost the level it had been just prior to World War 2. Yet while there was near-parity in the quantity of vessels on the run, the quality of the newer ships was, for the most part, far superior. For one thing, they were larger on average — both in tonnage and principal dimensions. In many cases they were faster too, but of greatest significance was that the overall standard of their accommodation — the appointments and the passenger facilities in all classes — was dramatically improved. This can be demonstrated by a few comparisons.

Cunard Line's new quartet of ships for the Montreal service were of similar tonnage and length to prewar vessels of the *Franconia* class but were half as big again as the 'A' class ships they had actually replaced. They were fast ships too at 22kt, and their passenger numbers of roughly 900, in contrast to the earlier class's 1,700, reveals an increase in capacity per

passenger of 190%. The four new vessels, *Ivernia, Saxonia, Carinthia* and *Sylvania*, entered service between September 1954 and June 1957, the former pair working from Southampton and the latter pair from Liverpool.

It was a similar story where Canadian Pacific was concerned. Two new Canadian Pacific passenger ships were introduced in the mid-1950s, the *Empress of England* and the *Empress of Britain*, the latter reviving the name of the company's most celebrated and majestic liner. In 1961 they were joined by the *Empress of Canada*, an even larger ship at 27,284 gross tons and 650ft overall length, being a developed version of the earlier pair. The three ships posed a real threat to the Cunarders, offering a healthy competitive choice to the prospective voyager. They also represented a massive leap in progress in all respects over the company's earlier vessels. Likewise, the ships of continental European operators reflected these advances.

Two elegant motor liners of the same names which were some 10-15% bigger than their predecessors filled the gap left

◄ The *Seven Seas* was one of the Tourist-class ships that operated on the Atlantic route from the 1950s. She had previously been the World War 2 auxiliary aircraft carrier *Long Island*. *Ian Shiffman*

by the disposal of Swedish America Line's old *Gripsholm* and *Kungsholm*. The third *Kungsholm* made her maiden voyage in November 1953, the second *Gripsholm* joining her in May 1957.

Norwegian America Line took delivery of a new *Bergensfjord* in May 1956. Generally similar to the *Oslofjord* of 1949, the later ship weighed 18,739 gross tons and measured 578ft in overall length. Together, the *Bergensfjord* and *Oslofjord* could convey a total of 1,500 passengers. Prior to 1939, the smaller old *Bergensfjord* and *Stavangerfjord* carried 2,300 between them. After the *Oslofjord* of 1938, which was sunk by mine in 1940, joined them the total passenger complement of the three ships increased to 3,150 — more than double that of the later, larger pair.

Both Swedish America and Norwegian America were to expand their fleets further still, with even bigger ships coming out in the 1960s.

Holland America was obliged to carry out an extensive modernisation programme, needing to make good the losses

of the *Statendam*, *Pennland*, *Westernland*, *Zaandam* (a torpedo victim) and the *Zuiderdam* which, sabotaged by the Dutch Resistance, was never completed.

To replace the last two ships, Holland America upgraded two cargo ships — the *Diemerdyk* and *Dinteldyk* — while they were still on the slipway, completing them as the *Maasdam* and *Ryndam* respectively. As adapted, they had tonnages of 15,000 gross. Because of their cargo-ship hulls, length, at 502ft, was rather short but they could carry 890 passengers in First and Tourist classes, working the route from Rotterdam to New York.

Almost simultaneously, Holland America brought out a new *Statendam* — the fourth of that name — a magnificent liner which, though predominantly Tourist-class, immediately elevated the Dutch concern's premier service. The *Statendam* worked alongside the *Nieuw Amsterdam*, the older ship being repainted in the pale grey hull colour that the new ship exhibited from the start. In 1959 the *Statendam* and *Nieuw Amsterdam* were complemented by the *Rotterdam*, a remarkable ship which was the largest liner the Holland America Line

had ever owned, at 38,645 gross tons. She was exquisitely appointed with a modern décor, sophisticated and restrained in its style and quite different from the brash and superficial modernity that featured aboard some of the other contemporary liners. Traditional funnel-shape exhausts were dispensed with, and in their place twin athwartship flutes were erected in a position further aft than was then common practice. This introduced a trend later adopted in P & O's *Canberra*, Costa Line's *Eugenio C.* and even for the projected but abandoned Cunard liner 'Q3'.

Another curious but cleverly innovative design feature of the *Rotterdam* was the arrangement of her intertwining main staircases. The First- and Tourist-class stairways occupied the same space and the passengers of either class passed by each other as they moved between decks but neither could access the public spaces of the other.

The *Volendam* and *Veendam* were retired respectively in 1952 and 1953. Like many other liners of their generation, they were making way for the new breed of ship which emerged in this decade.

For the Mediterranean route, American Export took delivery of the smart new liners *Constitution* and *Independence* in 1951. They were distinctive vessels, modern and fast but with design features that suggested the past — counter sterns and twin tall funnels, slightly tapered with rounded caps but otherwise reminiscent of an earlier period.

Rivalling the American operator was Italia with its elegant ships based at Genoa and, representing the new state of Israel, there was Zim Lines, inaugurated in 1953, whose home port was Haifa.

Italia Line had put two striking liners on the River Plate run in 1952 — the new *Augustus* and *Giulio Cesare*. Two years later, a larger pair, of broadly similar appearance, was commissioned for the North Atlantic service. They were the 29,000-ton *Andrea Doria* and *Cristoforo Colombo*.

Regrettably, the *Andrea Doria* survived for only three seasons, being lost in a catastrophic collision with Swedish America Line's *Stockholm*, 25 miles west of Nantucket on 25 July 1956. The two ships were travelling at speed, despite fog, the Italian ship inbound to New York, the Swedish vessel headed in an

▲ The *Nieuw Amsterdam*, showing the grey livery she wore during the final years of her career. *Ian Allan Library*

The *Vulcania* and her sister *Saturnia*, depicted here, continued in service on the Atlantic until 1965 when they were both 38 years old. The *Vulcania* was sold to Sicula Oceanica while the *Saturnia* was broken up. *Ian Shiffman*

Holland America's fourth *Statendam* entered service in 1957. Her accommodation was predominantly Tourist-class, reflecting the fast-growing trend towards this grade of fare. *Ian Shiffman*

easterly direction. The impact collapsed the *Stockholm*'s bow but she was in no danger of sinking. The *Andrea Doria*, on the other hand, was struck a fatal glancing blow, tearing an enormous hole in her side against which even the improved standard of watertight subdivision introduced following the *Titanic* tragedy could not provide protection. Distress signals brought the old *Ile de France* to the rescue but it was a close call for the sinking Italian ship and a major tragedy was only averted in the nick of time.

The loss of the *Andrea Doria* left Italia with only half of its transatlantic force, but an improved and enlarged ship of the same type was ordered in 1957, entering service as the *Leonardo da Vinci* on 30 June 1960. In the interim, the *Augustus* and *Giulio Cesare* supported the *Cristoforo Colombo* on the run.

Zim Lines' first ships, a series of small cargo passenger liners built in Germany as part of a war compensation package, were the *Zion*, *Israel* and *Jerusalem*. Each accommodated only 313 passengers, retaining a proportion of dormitory berths for

▲ The *Nieuw Amsterdam* and the modernistic *Rotterdam* together at the Rotterdam Drydock shipyard. *Rotterdamsche Droogdok Mij*

those emigrants of Jewish extraction who, despite the establishment of an independent homeland, still preferred to make their future in North America.

A characteristic of the 1950s was the extensive availability of emigrant and inexpensive Tourist-grade berths. Home Lines and Greek Line have been mentioned earlier; added to these was a Swiss-flag operation, the Arosa Line. On the emigrant front, passages for this grade of passenger could in fact be obtained on a range of small, mostly converted ships.

The Dutch Government had placed three converted Victory ships in the trade from 1951, the *Zuiderkruis*, *Groote Beer* and *Waterman*. Each could accommodate 800 passengers, again in very basic quarters. Two other wartime conversions were the broadly similar *Roma* and *Sydney* which Lauro Lines temporarily placed on the run, this pair having been converted from escort carriers, though they had started life as freighters. There was also Europe Canada Line's *Seven Seas*, perhaps the most enduring of these small emigrant carriers, plus a number of other vessels of this type which came and went for brief periods.

Another Dutch company, the Oranje Line, entered the

Atlantic passenger business in 1953 with the *Prins Willem Van Oranje*, which had limited, First-class-only space for just 60 passengers. Six years later the stylish *Prinses Irene* came out, followed, in 1961, by a sister vessel, the *Prinses Margriet*. Accommodation was increased to 115 passengers each aboard these ships, which worked the St Lawrence route, continuing beyond Montreal and Quebec as far as the Great Lakes.

Meanwhile, Home Lines had added to its original foursome with more second-hand tonnage. The *Homeric* (ex-*Mariposa*) commenced sailings out of Southampton in May 1955, relieving the *Atlantic* which then transferred to a Piraeus to New York route, renamed *Queen Frederika*. Home Lines took the opportunity presented by the *Homeric*'s arrival to pay off the *Brasil*; the *Argentina* had been sold on to Zim Lines three years earlier. The *Homeric* achieved a postwar record by crossing from Rimouski to Le Havre in 1956 at an average speed marginally above 22kt.

Greek Line added two striking vessels to its fleet in the 1950s. The purpose-built *Olympia* entered service in 1953 and five years later was joined by the *Arkadia*, formerly an Australian

The Arosa Line's first ships were relatively small, such as the *Arosa Kulm* — a ship with a multi-faceted past.
Ian Allan Library

emigrant ship but originally the Furness Bermuda liner *Monarch of Bermuda* which had been severely damaged in a fire in 1947 while undergoing a refit on the River Tyne. The pair strengthened Greek Line's presence on the North Atlantic, the *Arkadia* operating out of North European ports, and the *Olympia* working the Mediterranean route from 1955. The *Olympia* and *Arkadia* were predominantly Tourist ships — indeed the *Olympia* was specifically designed to cater for this grade of passenger — but much of their accommodation was interchangeable, allowing the small number of First-class cabins to be increased whenever it was expedient.

Hinting at what Freddie Laker was to later attempt with low-cost airline travel, the Arosa Line commenced operations in 1952 offering very competitively-priced Tourist passages. Unfortunately, the company could not sustain itself with such small margins on its revenues and went out of business after just six seasons. Four ships carried the buff and black colours of the short-lived company. There were the *Arosa Kulm*, a much-transferred vessel which had seen service under five different flags, the *Arosa Star* (ex-*Puerto Rico*), and the *Arosa Sun*

▲ The *Arosa Sun*, formerly Messageries Maritimes' *Felix Roussel*, made her first Arosa Line voyage from Trieste to New York, beginning 14 July 1955. *Ian Allan Library*

◄ Prior to entering service for Arosa Line, the *Arosa Sky* had served as the French Navy hospital ship *La Marseillaise* at Suez. *Ian Allan Library*

American Export had the *Independence* and *Constitution* repainted with grey hulls in 1959, at the same time as they were substantially modified to increase the capacity of their passenger accommodation.
Ian Shiffman

The *Cristoforo Colombo*, sister ship to the ill-fated *Andrea Doria*; a spectacular view of her at speed, her decks crowded with passengers.
Ian Allan Library

which had formerly been the *Felix Roussel* of Messageries Maritimes — one of the strange square-funnelled ships which that company brought out in the 1930s. Best of the Arosa ships was another former Messageries Maritimes vessel, the *Arosa Sky* (ex-*La Marseillaise*), which was taken over after a brief spell as a hospital ship during the Suez emergency. Although fare-rates on the *Arosa Sky* were set at a higher level than on the earlier Arosa vessels, it made little difference to the company's fortunes.

Having reinstated its premier service, French Line introduced just one new ship on the North Atlantic route during the 1950s. This was the strikingly-designed *Flandre*, one of a pair, the sister vessel *Antilles* being placed on the run from Le Havre to the West Indies. These 20,000-ton liners were comparable in size to Cunard's *Ivernia* class, but their low, racy profile, topped off by a long, squat funnel with a rounded dome, gave them the impression of being rather smaller. Introduction of the *Flandre*, replacing the old *De Grasse* which became Canadian Pacific's *Empress of Australia*, allowed the French Line to implement a schedule of weekly sailings from Le Havre to New York, but, with three quite different ships, it was an unbalanced service.

Germany finally returned to the Atlantic with a succession of revamped second-hand ships acquired from other companies. First out was the *Berlin* (ex-*Gripsholm*), jointly owned with Swedish America Line. Looking smart in her Norddeutscher Lloyd colours, she entered the Gothenburg, Bremerhaven and New York service in January 1955, ending a 14-year absence. By 1959, when Norddeutscher Lloyd took total ownership of the *Berlin*, it complemented her with a new *Bremen*, the former *Pasteur* of Compagnie de Navigation Sud-Atlantique. Built for the La Plata service from Bordeaux, the *Pasteur* was prevented from making even her maiden voyage on this run because of the outbreak of war. Five years of

The *Zion*, shown here, and *Israel* were slightly larger cargo-passenger ships which maintained a regular Atlantic service for Zim Israel Line.
Alex Duncan

The *Theodor Herzl* and her sister *Jerusalem* were intended for the Haifa to Marseilles service, but made occasional voyages across the Atlantic to New York.
Ian Allan Library

The new *Statendam*, completed in 1957.
Ian Allan Library

trooping under the British flag were followed by 12 more under the Tricolor. The *Pasteur* was a misfit with no obvious future from 1957 when she was laid up until she was rescued by Norddeutscher Lloyd for conversion into its splendid new flagship, extensively modernised and fitted out for 216 First-class and 906 Tourist-class passengers.

Just prior to the emergence of the *Bremen*, the even more drastically-restyled *Empress of Scotland* re-entered the Atlantic service as the *Hanseatic* for the Hamburg Atlantic line. Hamburg Atlantic, later restyled as the German Atlantic Line, had associations with the Home Lines but was also funded in part by the city where the company was based. The *Hanseatic*, a predominantly Tourist-class ship, was almost unrecognisable as her former self, with

two vividly-coloured funnels, later fitted
with smoke deflection cowls, in place of her
original three. Though a lone ship, the
Hanseatic was an extraordinarily popular and
profitable vessel, working between
Cuxhaven, Le Havre, Southampton and New
York.

In November 1958, a final *au revoir* was
bade to the *Ile de France* when she completed
her final voyage from New York. She had
truly opened the modern era on the Atlantic,
and her passing took place at a critical time
for the transatlantic passenger trade. Just a
month earlier, the very first regular jet airline
service to London had been started, reducing
the crossing time from days to hours.

Within a year there were as many
passengers travelling by air between the Old
and New Worlds as there were by sea. The
writing was on the wall.

The second of Canadian Pacific's new postwar passenger liners, the *Empress of England*. *Ian Allan Library*

The second *Gripsholm* at New York. *Worldship Photo Library*

When the former *Empress of Scotland* re-emerged in July 1958 as the *Hanseatic* she was almost unrecognisable. Another Tourist-class ship, she was popular throughout her brief career under the German flag. *Deutsches Schiffahrtsmuseum*

▲ Greek Line added the *Queen Anna Maria* — previously Canadian Pacific's *Empress of Britain* — to its fleet of Atlantic ships in 1965 as a replacement for the *Arkadia*, which was disposed of a year later. *Ian Shiffman*

◄ Greek Line's *Arkadia*, originally the three-funnelled *Monarch of Bermuda*. *Ian Allan Library*

9. WESTERN OCEAN DECLINE — THE END OF AN ERA

The year 1958 witnessed the number of passengers crossing the Atlantic by ship reach its highest level ever. For the first and only time, the figure exceeded 1,200,000 — a quite incredible volume which stands out all the more when viewed against the totals for other, earlier periods. It is greater, for instance, than the total passengers recorded for 1914, the high-point of the Atlantic trade before World War 1, when the emigrant traffic was at its busiest. Also, the 1958 figure is almost 200,000 higher than the best of the interwar years, 1929, when, prior to the collapse precipitated by the Wall Street crash, 1,069,000 passengers crossed the Atlantic. From that point, the number of occupied berths collapsed drastically, reaching its lowest ebb in 1934 at just 460,000.

The record passenger numbers of 1958 were achieved 118 years after regular Atlantic steamship schedules had been first established. More importantly, though, when viewed in retrospect, they were achieved barely 15 years before the transatlantic passenger liner business all but disappeared altogether. The speed and intensity of the decline which followed this high-point was staggering. In a sense it over-whelmed operators, making it almost impossible for them to react effectively to events unfolding at this pace. They had no way of knowing whether the decline was temporary or permanent, whether the ocean liner would be rendered completely extinct or whether this spectacular fall would bottom out at some level which would leave a continuing need for Atlantic ships in some shape or form.

Identifying the cause of the collapse was easy enough: it was the jet-engined commercial airliner. Countering it, however, was a totally different proposition. Just one year after jet aircraft schedules across the Atlantic were inaugurated, as many people were travelling by this means of transportation as were still crossing by ship. Seven years later, occupancy levels on the ships had dropped below what they had been 1931 — a time when Atlantic travel was adversely affected by the ravages of the Great Depression. By 1969, over 6 million passengers annually were taking flights, five times more than the record number of ship passengers of only 11 years earlier. All this rather takes the gloss off that pinnacle of achievement of the postwar years. One thing was for certain as the 1950s drew to a close: the Atlantic liner's glory days would, it seemed, soon be over.

◀◀ The *Leonardo da Vinci* replaced the *Andrea Doria*. She is seen in the Panama Canal when already partially diverted from the North Atlantic service. Her hull was originally painted black. *Italia Line*

◀ An *Alexandr Pushkin*-class liner at Southampton's New Docks in July 1986. These ships were late entrants on the Atlantic routes to both Montreal and New York. *David L. Williams*

The *Rotterdam* introduced many novel design features, both internally and externally, the most distinctive being the absence of conventional funnels.
Tom Rayner

▲ When technology changes at this sort of rate, it is doubtful whether anything can be done effectively to alter the course of events. Nevertheless, the degree to which the threat posed by long-haul airliners was underestimated is quite astonishing. Few people in positions of influence, even so-called experts, had the vision to perceive a future where the ocean passenger liner could be totally displaced, a completely obsolete form of transport. Back in the 1920s, when the following, uncredited remarks were expressed, it was very different. Typifying the contemporary view, air travel was seen as no more than a novelty:

'The simple truth is that aerial transport can never be made to pay. It can only be run on a scale of charges, which, compared with stateroom fares, is simply preposterous. Flying has come to stay but I cannot believe that the airway will ever replace the seaway. We can step aboard a Cunarder at either Southampton or Liverpool with a feeling of assurance that we shall be in New York with time-table punctuality, travelling in luxury and safety. The aircraft can never hold such assurance.'

While this was, no doubt, fair comment for that time, unfortunately it reflected attitudes that were still to some extent regarded as valid long after the war, revealing an acute absence of foresight. The industry failed to heed the words of another, more accurate maritime prophet who addressed the same subject some 20 years later. In an uncannily-accurate, almost Huxley-like prediction of the future, James L. Bates, then the Director of the Technical Division of the United States Maritime Commission, revealed that, for some at least, the realisation of what lay ahead was beginning to dawn:

'During the half dozen years immediately succeeding the present conflict [World War 2], all facilities for passenger transport, whether air, water or land, probably will be utilised to capacity. Later, air travel should attract more and more of the available First-class passengers, principally because of its superior speed which is a permanent and compelling advantage over other forms of passenger transport. Ultimately, it is believed that the water transport of passengers will be so decreased as to become rather a minor factor outside of the "cruise" for relaxation and recreation.'

In practical terms, just as predicted, as passengers were increasingly attracted on to aircraft, the number of ships on the transatlantic routes quickly reduced, while for those that remained, the level of utilisation was cut. Also, as forecast, the

◄ Norddeutscher Lloyd's new *Bremen* (ex-*Pasteur*), another ship which underwent an elaborate reconstruction, dramatically altering her appearance. *Hapag Lloyd*

▼ The *Empress of Canada*, last of a long line of elegant Canadian Pacific 'Empress' liners, undergoing speed trials in the Firth of Clyde in March 1961. *Ian Allan Library*

impact of air travel was initially a phenomenon that affected First-class passengers, perhaps because, initially, air fares were not sufficiently competitive to be affordable by all. Thus the Tourist traffic held out the longest.

The first casualties of all this were the older vessels which did not cater predominantly for the cheaper end of the market. The last White Star liner, the *Britannic*, was retired in December 1960, a year which also witnessed the passing of the *Empress of France*, to the scrapyard, and the *Stockholm*, which was sold to an East German Trades Union organisation for full-time cruising.

In 1961, retirements included the *Liberté* (ex-*Europa*), which went for scrap in Italy, and the Greek Line's *New York*, the last of the former Anchor Line transatlantic ships, which was broken up after two years of idleness, laid up at Piraeus. The Cunarders *Media* and *Parthia* and the small Furness Warren ships *Newfoundland* and *Nova Scotia* were all sold to new owners for continued trading on other sea routes. The *Flandre* was moved to the West Indies route where she remained for six years prior to conversion for full-time cruising. The most notable disposal of 1963 was the old *Stavangerfjord*, then 45 years old, which had completed 770 Atlantic crossings over her long career.

When the Atlantic schedules collapsed, the *Rotterdam* was saved by adaptation for cruising. Later in her career her hull was painted dark blue. *Author's collection*

The final *Bremen*. She looked particularly smart in the colours of Norddeutscher Lloyd but her Atlantic career was short-lived. *Ian Shiffman*

These reductions were partially offset by new ships, five in all, among them the *Empress of Canada* in April 1961 and the new French Line flagship *France* in 1962. From this point, however, the decline on the Atlantic began to gather momentum. Any operators who until then had mistakenly believed that the airliner's threat had been weathered were about to experience a sharp reminder that the trade really would never be the same again. The 64 ships that had been on the run in 1957 had reduced to just under 50 and the alarm bells were beginning to ring.

In 1963, two of Cunard's St Lawrence service ships were withdrawn and converted for dedicated cruise operations. The *Ivernia* was renamed *Franconia* while the *Saxonia* became the *Carmania*. Both received a changed colour scheme like that of the *Caronia*. In February of 1964 the *Queen Elizabeth* made the first ever cruise by either of the 'Queens', as their scheduled passenger numbers plummeted. It was said at the time that these superb ships were making crossings virtually empty, the crew members often exceeding the number of fare-paying passengers.

The nature of the changes sweeping the transatlantic passenger trade were, by this time, manifesting themselves not just as an impact on individual ships but, more sinisterly, at the fleet level. In 1962, Canadian Pacific had discontinued its winter sailings to Canada altogether, sending its ships, including the one-year-old *Empress of Canada*, on luxury cruises. At the same time, for the remaining eight months of the year, the company's schedule was cut to just two departures every three weeks.

Earlier still, in 1959, the Greek Line had suspended its Bremerhaven to New York service. Home Lines quit the North Atlantic passenger business completely in 1963 and just three years later Greek Line followed suit with the discontinuation of its Montreal service. The *Homeric* was re-employed as a permanent cruise ship, partnering a new liner, the *Oceanic*, which had been in part conceived for the scheduled passenger service but which never made a single line voyage.

By the mid-1960s, with the parting of top-flight vessels like the *America*, it was clear that the transatlantic trade was in freefall. It was becoming increasingly obvious, too, that the

▲ The *Shalom*, Zim Line's bold investment in a new flagship, had little opportunity to recover her cost. By the time she entered service, the Atlantic passenger business from the eastern Mediterranean had evaporated. After only three years she was sold to the German Atlantic Line.
Ian Shiffman

Swedish America's last and finest *Kungsholm* arriving at Pier 57, New York, at the end of her maiden voyage in April 1966. *Ian Allan Library*

German Atlantic Line, as it had been restyled, replaced the old *Hanseatic* (ex-*Empress of Scotland*) with another *Hanseatic*, the former *Shalom*. *Deutsche Atlantik Linie*

downward curve would not flatten out at some point or, more remotely, turn up again as the ocean liner, in some adapted form, would bounce back. The number of ships on the route was down to half the number of eight years earlier, and those that were still operating were spending more and more time cruising — an activity on which their continued viability largely depended.

The problem was that cruising, as a fill-in alternative when business was flat, was not the solution, and certainly not for the older ships. Cunard had experimented with the *Mauretania*, repositioning her in the Mediterranean and committing her to a full-time cruise programme from 1963. Two years later, it was accepted that this had failed and she was sent for scrap. Cruising gave the *Sylvania* and *Carinthia* a brief reprieve but, hastened by the National Union of Seamen's strike in 1966, they were laid up prior to entering the Australian emigrant trade for new owners. The *Sylvania* had, in fact, played a poignant rôle in bringing the curtain down on part of Cunard's line operations. Her departure from the River Mersey on 24 November 1966 brought to an end the Liverpool to New York sailings which Cunard had inaugurated way back in 1848.

The unfolding events of the transatlantic trade during the 1960s, as the business continued to run down, make for depressing reading, though this should never be regarded as a detrimental reflection on the marvellous ships that had maintained the service for so long. Besides which, it was not all one-way traffic, anyway. Some exciting new ships were still entering service in this period, among them Zim Line's elegant *Shalom*, the largest passenger liner owned by the youthful Israeli concern. Completed in 1964, she went on to serve with the German Atlantic Line, replacing the old *Hanseatic* which was destroyed by fire. Rechristened with the same name, the new *Hanseatic* continued, first as a dual-rôle liner and then as a dedicated cruise ship, for another six years.

A year after the *Shalom*, Italia Line introduced the *Michelangelo* and *Raffaello* on the Mediterranean route and, as the peak in the evolution of Norwegian America Line's fleet, the *Sagafjord* entered the service from Oslo to New York. This was the first of two similar and significantly larger vessels; the later ship of the pair, the *Vistafjord*, never worked on the Atlantic run.

In 1966, as a sign of relaxing East/West attitudes, the Soviet Union placed ships on the Atlantic service for the first time. The national shipping line took delivery of five modern, East German-built liners between 1964 and 1972. Attractively proportioned, though with a rather basic single grade of

The *Stefan Batory* (ex-*Maasdam*) of Polish Ocean Lines in the St Lawrence Seaway. By 1976, she was one of only two ships remaining on the Atlantic run, the other being the *Queen Elizabeth 2*. *Ian Shiffman*

The *Kungsholm* survived on a mixture of cruises and infrequent Atlantic crossings until August 1975. She was eventually sold to P & O for conversion into the cruise ship *Sea Princess*. *Ian Shiffman*

accommodation, they were intended initially for operation on established Russian domestic routes. From the spring of 1966, the *Alexandr Pushkin*, second of the class, entered the Montreal service from Leningrad (now renamed St Petersburg). Sailings continued through to 1975 but the schedules omitted the winter months, when the St Lawrence was frozen over. In May 1973, the *Alexandr Pushkin*'s sister ship, the *Mikhail Lermontov*, breached the biggest embargo when she commenced an irregular service into New York.

Swedish America Line's fourth, last and finest *Kungsholm* made her maiden voyage in April 1966. At the time of her construction she was the largest and most powerful motor liner in the world. She was a dual-rôle vessel, working on the Gothenburg to New York route for part of the year and making luxury cruises for the remainder of the season. An impressive and stylish liner, she constituted the closest her owners were to get to realising a ship of similar size and quality to the large *Stockholm* lost in World War 2.

It has to be said that the better developments in this period were only transitory. They were but brief interludes in an otherwise downward spiral in the Atlantic passenger business. As if to reinforce this, there occurred in 1967 probably the most emphatic confirmation of the negative direction in which the trade was headed when, that October, the most legendary of the great ocean liners of the 20th century, the *Queen Mary*, was paid off. Fortunately, she was spared the cutter's torch, purchased instead for permanent retention as a monument to the age of the ocean liners, berthed at Long Beach, California, where she would double as a hotel and convention centre. It is regrettable that the British, whose creation she was, did not have as strong a

The *United States* in drydock at the Norfolk Shipbuilding yard at the time when cancelled subsidies caused the abrupt termination of her Atlantic career.
Norfolk Shipbuilding Corp

Towed away to be laid up pending decisions on her future, the *United States* had her funnels repainted on the port side only, such was the swiftness of the 'stop work' order. Thirty years later she remains idle, the prospects for reactivation diminishing as the years advance.
Norfolk Shipbuilding Corp

▲ sense of tradition as the Americans. The fact that no concerted effort was made to find a permanent resting place for the *Queen Mary* in the United Kingdom — on Clydebank or at Southampton — is an enduring tragedy.

A similar retirement was planned for the *Queen Elizabeth* when she was retired in 1968 but, in her case, the preservation scheme (again in the United States) did not unfold quite as fortuitously. A subsequent project to convert her into an international university of the sea looked hopeful but she was destroyed by fire at Hong Kong just prior to readiness to commence her new duties.

The list of vessels being withdrawn from the Atlantic service was now escalating rapidly, comprising no fewer than

14 between 1966 and 1968 and including, besides the two 'Queens', the *Caronia*, *Independence* and *Constitution*. It seemed that it would not be long before the route would be abandoned altogether. Those route voyages that were still being made could have barely been profitable with a large percentage of the available berths unoccupied.

In November 1969 the *United States* was undergoing her annual overhaul at the Norfolk Shipbuilding (Norshipco) yard when the United States Government voted to withdraw the ship's operating subsidy — she had been costing the American taxpayer $12 million per annum. Even with this level of financial support, her owners were still losing another $5 million each year. The United States Lines was left with no

choice but to terminate operation of the liner with immediate effect. So swift was the enforcement of the decision that her refit was abruptly stopped. The *United States* was unceremoniously removed from floating dock and towed away. As an indication of the speed of the work stoppage, her funnels were left only half-painted. The *United States* would never again cross the Atlantic.

That same season, Cunard's new flagship, the *Queen Elizabeth 2*, entered service. Despite the celebration surrounding her début, there was underlying concern as to how she would fare. The *Queen Elizabeth 2* was never a true Atlantic liner, although it was intended that she would complete so many round voyages each year. Mostly, though, she was to be employed on luxury cruises, but it was to be some time before she carved out for herself a reputation as the most

prestigious cruise ship in the world. For too long she regularly lost her owners £500,000 year after year, causing Cunard Line itself to become the victim of these difficult times. The company passed into the ownership of Trafalgar House Investments before the *Queen Elizabeth 2*'s balance sheet went from red into the black.

As the 1960s drew to a close, there were only eight operators left working the Atlantic service, with less than a dozen ships between them — none of them making scheduled sailings full-time. Of these companies, Holland America and Norddeutscher Lloyd withdrew in September 1971, the Canadian Pacific Line following suit in November the same year. The French Line held out for three years but laid up the *France* in September 1974, after a dispute with her crew acted as the catalyst for this difficult decision. Her future was later

The last liner intended for a measure of Atlantic work, the *Queen Elizabeth 2* has in fact extended the history of the Western Ocean passenger trade for another quarter of a century, virtually single-handed. *Skyfotos*

▲ assured when she was purchased for conversion into the cruise ship *Norway*.

When Swedish America Line abandoned the Atlantic service in December 1975 and the Italia Line did the same in June 1976 — the *Michelangelo* and *Raffaello* became Iranian Navy accommodation ships — the only liners left operating on the Atlantic were the *Queen Elizabeth 2* and the *Stefan Batory* (ex-*Maasdam*); these would continue for a few years more. In fact, the *Queen Elizabeth 2* continues to make infrequent — some might say token — Atlantic voyages each year, in association with fly holidays to North America.

The airliner did not, in the event, wipe out the ocean passenger ship, but it did completely destroy its scheduled operations. With them went the glamour and ambience of a very special form of travel which today's cruise ships, despite the ever-improving quality of their accommodation and public facilities, can never match.

Apart from the *Queen Mary*, sadly very little of a tangible nature is now left of the great age of Atlantic liner travel. However, today's highly active market in ocean liner memorabilia of all descriptions — everything from menus, posters, crockery, baggage labels and all manner of fixtures and fittings — suggests that there is an enduring nostalgia for this magical era when the transatlantic liners enjoyed their Glory Days.

APPENDIX I: THE ATLANTIC BLUE RIBAND SPEED RECORD HOLDERS 1920–1970

Ship		Date	Average Speed	Ship		Date	Average Speed
Mauretania	(GB)	(September 1910)	**26.06kt** Westbound	*Queen Mary*	(GB)	August 1936	**30.14kt** Westbound
		August 1924	**27.03kt** Eastbound			August 1936	**30.63kt** Eastbound
Bremen	(D)	July 1929	**27.83kt** Westbound	*Normandie*	(F)	July 1937	**30.58kt** Westbound
		July 1929	**27.92kt** Eastbound			August 1937	**31.20kt** Eastbound
Europa	(D)	March 1930	**27.91kt** Westbound	*Queen Mary*	(GB)	August 1938	**30.99kt** Westbound
Bremen	(D)	July 1933	**28.51kt** Westbound			August 1938	**31.69kt** Eastbound
Rex	(I)	August 1933	**28.92kt** Westbound	*United States*	(USA)	July 1952	**34.51kt** Westbound
Normandie	(F)	May 1935	**29.98kt** Westbound			July 1952	**35.59kt** Eastbound
		June 1935	**30.31kt** Eastbound				

◀ Luxury Liner Row, New York, on 3 July 1961. Once the home of the ocean liner, it is now largely deserted of these magnificent vessels. Miami is now the USA's premier passenger port, thronging with cruise ships of all sizes and national flags. Among the liners on view here are the *Queen Elizabeth, United States, Independence, Olympia, America* and *Mauretania*.
Port of New York Authority — William Miller

NB: Listed ships are liners employed predominantly on the North Atlantic with substantial, permanent passenger accommodation (100+)

1937

	GRT	LOA
Alaunia (Cunard White Star)	14,030	538ft / 164.0m
Andania (Cunard White Star)	13,950	538ft / 164.0m
Antonia (Cunard White Star)	13,867	540ft / 164.6m
Aquitania (Cunard White Star)	45,647	901ft / 274.8m
Ascania (Cunard White Star)	14,013	538ft / 164.1m
Athenia (Donaldson Line)	13,465	538ft / 164.0m
Augustus (Italia)	30,418	711ft / 216.6m
Aurania (Cunard White Star)	13,984	540ft / 164.6m
Ausonia (Cunard White Star)	13,912	538ft / 164.0m
Batory (Gdynia America)	14,287	526ft / 160.3m
Berengaria (Cunard White Star)	52,226	909ft / 277.1m
Bergensfjord (Norwegian America)	11,015	530ft / 161.5m
Berlin (Norddeutscher Lloyd)	15,286	572ft / 174.3m
Bremen (Norddeutscher Lloyd)	51,731	938ft / 286.0m
Britannic (Cunard White Star)	26,943	712ft / 217.0m
Caledonia (Anchor)	17,046	578ft / 176.2m
California (Anchor)	16,792	579ft / 176.5m
Cameronia (Anchor)	16,297	578ft / 176.3m
Carinthia (Cunard White Star)	20,277	624ft / 190.2m
Champlain (French Line)	28,124	641ft / 195.4m
Columbus (Norddeutscher Lloyd)	32,565	775ft / 236.2m
Conte di Savoia (Italia)	48,502	860ft / 262.2m
Deutschland (Hamburg Amerika)	21,046	677ft / 206.3m
Drottningholm (Swedish America)	11,182	538ft / 164.0m
Duchess of Atholl (Canadian Pacific)	20,119	601ft / 183.2m
Duchess of Bedford (Canadian Pacific)	20,123	601ft / 183.1m
Duchess of Richmond (Canadian Pacific)	20,022	601ft / 183.1m
Duchess of York (Canadian Pacific)	20,021	601ft / 183.1m
Empress of Australia (Canadian Pacific)	21,833	615ft / 187.4m
Empress of Britain (Canadian Pacific)	42,348	760ft / 231.8m
Europa (Norddeutscher Lloyd)	49,746	941ft / 286.7m
Excalibur (American Export)	9,359	474ft / 144.5m
Excambion (American Export)	9,360	474ft / 144.5m
Exeter (American Export)	9,360	474ft / 144.5m
Exochorda (American Export)	9,359	474ft / 144.5m
Franconia (Cunard White Star)	20,175	623ft / 190.0m
Georgic (Cunard White Star)	27,759	711ft / 216.7m
Gripsholm (Swedish America)	18,134	573ft / 174.6m
Hamburg (Hamburg Amerika)	22,117	677ft / 206.5m
Hansa (Hamburg Amerika)	21,131	677ft / 206.3m
Ile de France (French Line)	43,450	792ft / 241.3m
Kungsholm (Swedish America)	20,067	609ft / 185.6m
Laconia (Cunard White Star)	19,695	623ft / 190.0m
Lafayette (French Line)	25,178	613ft / 186.8m
Lancastria (Cunard White Star)	16,243	578ft / 176.3m
Letitia (Donaldson)	13,475	538ft / 164.0m
Manhattan (United States Lines)	24,289*	705ft / 214.9m
Milwaukee (Hamburg Amerika)	16,699	575ft / 175.1m
Montcalm (Canadian Pacific)	16,418	575ft / 175.3m
Montclare (Canadian Pacific)	16,314	575ft / 175.3m
Montrose (Canadian Pacific)	16,402	575ft / 175.3m
Newfoundland (Furness Warren)	6,791	423ft / 129.0m
New York (Hamburg Amerika)	22,337	677ft / 206.5m
Normandie (French Line)	83,423	1,029ft / 313.7m
Nova Scotia (Furness Warren)	6,796	423ft / 129.0m
Paris (French Line)	34,569	764ft / 233.0m
Pennland (Bernstein Red Star)	16,332	600ft / 182.9m
Pilsudski (Gdynia America)	14,294	526ft / 160.3m
President Harding (United States Lines)	13,869	535ft / 163.1m
President Roosevelt (United States Lines)	13,869	535ft / 163.1m
Queen Mary (Cunard White Star)	81,235	1,019ft / 310.5m
Rex (Italia)	51,062	880ft / 268.2m
Roma (Italia)	32,583	709ft / 216.1m
Rotterdam (Holland America)	24,149	667ft / 203.2m
Samaria (Cunard White Star)	19,597	624ft / 190.2m
Saturnia (Italia)	24,470	632ft / 192.5m
Scythia (Cunard White Star)	19,761	624ft / 190.2m
Statendam (Holland America)	28,291	697ft / 212.5m
Stavangerfjord (Nowegian America)	13,156	553ft / 168.5m
St. Louis (Hamburg Amerika)	16,732	574ft / 174.9m
Transylvania (Anchor)	16,923	575ft / 175.3m
Tuscania (Anchor)	16,991	580ft / 176.8m
Veendam (Holland America)	15,450	579ft / 176.5m
Volendam (Holland America)	15,434	572ft / 175.6m
Vulcania (Italia)	24,469	632ft / 192.5m
Washington (United States Lines)	24,289*	705ft / 214.9m
Westernland (Bernstein Red Star)	16,314	601ft / 183.1m

TOTAL = 77 ships

1957

	GRT	LOA		GRT	LOA
America (United States Lines)	26,314*	723ft / 220.4m	*Neptunia* (Greek Line)	10,519	523ft / 159.4m
Arosa Sky (Arosa)	17,321	593ft / 180.8m	*Newfoundland* (Furness Warren)	7,437	440ft / 134.1m
Arosa Star (Arosa)	7,114	465ft / 141.8m	**New York** (Greek Line)	16,991	580ft / 176.8m
Arosa Sun (Arosa)	20,126	600ft / 183.0m	*Nieuw Amsterdam* (Holland America)	36,667	759ft / 231.2m
Ascania (Siosa)	9,536	511ft / 155.8m	*Noordam* (Holland America)	10,276	502ft / 152.9m
Augustus (Italia)	27,090	680ft / 207.3m	*Nova Scotia* (Furness Warren)	7,438	440ft / 134.1m
Batory (Polish Ocean)	14,287	526ft / 160.3m	*Olympia* (Greek Line)	22,979	612ft / 186.5m
Bergensfjord (Norwegian America)	18,739	578ft / 176.2m	*Oslofjord* (Norwegian America)	16,844	577ft / 175.9m
Berlin (Norddeutscher Lloyd)	18,600	590ft / 179.8m	*Parthia* (Cunard)	13,362	532ft / 162.1m
Britannic (Cunard)	27,666	712ft / 217.0m	*Queen Elizabeth* (Cunard)	83,673	1,031ft / 314.3m
Carinthia (Cunard)	21,947	608ft / 185.3m	*Queen Frederica* (Home Lines)	20,553	582ft / 177.3m
Caronia (Cunard)	34,172	715ft / 217.9m	**Queen Mary** (Cunard)	81,237	1,019ft / 310.5m
Castel Felice (Sitmar)	12,150	493ft / 150.3m	*Ryndam* (Holland America)	15,015	502ft / 153.2m
Columbia (Greek Line)	9,424	466ft / 142.1m	**Saturnia** (Italia)	23,346	632ft / 192.5m
Constitution (American Export)	23,754*	682ft / 208.0m	*Saxonia* (Cunard)	21,637	608ft / 185.3m
Cristoforo Colombo (Italia)	29,191	700ft / 213.4m	**Scythia** (Cunard)	19,930	624ft / 190.2m
Empress of Britain (Canadian Pacific)	25,516	640ft / 195.1m	*Seven Seas* (Europe Canada)	12,575	492ft / 150.0m
Empress of England (Canadian Pacific)	25,585	640ft / 195.0m	*Skaubryn* (Greek Line)	9,786	458ft / 139.6m
Empress of France (Canadian Pacific)	20,448	601ft / 183.1m	*Statendam* (Holland America)	24,294	642ft / 195.8m
Empress of Scotland (Canadian Pacific)	26,313	666ft / 203.1m	**Stavangerfjord** (Norwegian America)	13,156	553ft / 168.5m
Excalibur (American Export)	9,644	473ft / 144.2m	*Stockholm* (Swedish America)	12,644	525ft / 160.1m
Excambion (American Export)	9,644	473ft / 144.2m	*Sylvania* (Cunard)	21,989	608ft / 185.3m
Exeter (American Export)	9,644	473ft / 144.2m	*United States* (United States Lines)	53,329	990ft / 301.8m
Exochorda (American Export)	9,644	473ft / 144.2m	**Vulcania** (Italia)	24,496	632ft / 192.5m
Fairsea (Sitmar)	13,432	492ft / 150.0m	*Waterman* (Netherlands Govt)	9,177	455ft / 138.7m
Flandre (French Line)	20,469	600ft / 182.8m	*Westerdam* (Holland America)	12,149	518ft / 157.9m
Giulio Cesare (Italia)	27,078	681ft / 207.6m	*Zion* (Zim)	9,855	501ft / 152.7m
Gripsholm (Swedish America)	23,191	631ft / 192.3m	*Zuiderkruis* (Netherlands Govt)	9,126	455ft / 138.7m
Groote Beer (Netherlands Govt)	9,191	455ft / 138.7m			
Homeric (Home)	18,563	641ft / 195.5m			
Ile de France (French Line)	44,356	792ft / 241.3m			
Independence (American Export)	23,719*	682ft / 208.0m			
Israel (Zim)	9,831	501ft / 152.7m			
Italia (Home)	21,532	609ft / 185.6m			
Ivernia (Cunard)	21,717	608ft / 185.3m			
Kungsholm (Swedish America)	21,141	600ft / 182.9m			
Liberté (French Line)	51,839	941ft / 286.7m			
Maasdam (Holland America)	15,024	502ft / 153.2m			
Mauretania (Cunard)	35,677	772ft / 235.4m			
Media (Cunard)	13,345	531ft / 162.0m			

TOTAL = 68 ships

Notes:

1. Liners in the 1937 column whose names are underlined were sunk or destroyed during World War 2.
2. Liners which appear in both columns have their names emboldened.
3. The gross tonnage of liners marked * was greater according to alternative systems of measurement:

America	33,532	*Manhattan*	(29,600)
Constitution	30,293	*Washington*	29,627
Independence	30,293		

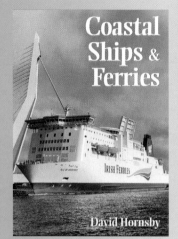
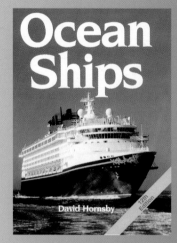
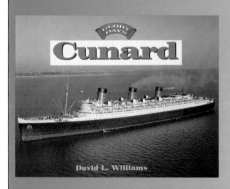
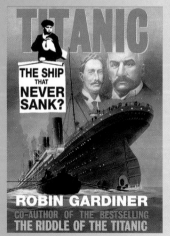